PROLIFERATION CONTROL REGIMES:
BACKGROUND AND STATUS

Proliferation Control Regimes: Background and Status

Sharon A. Squassoni, Steven R. Bowman
and Carl E. Behrens

Novinka Books
New York

Senior Editors: Susan Boriotti and Donna Dennis
Coordinating Editor: Tatiana Shohov
Office Manager: Annette Hellinger
Graphics: Wanda Serrano
Editorial Production: Vladimir Klestov, Matthew Kozlowski and Maya Columbus
Circulation: Ave-Maria Gonzalez, Vera Popovic, Luis Aviles, Raymond Davis, Melissa Diaz and Jeannie Pappas
Communications and Acquisitions: Serge P. Shohov
Marketing: Cathy DeGregory

Library of Congress Cataloging-in-Publication Data
Available Upon Request

ISBN: 1-59033-559-7.

Copyright © 2002 by Novinka Books
Nova Science Publishers, Inc.
400 Oser Ave, Suite 1600
Hauppauge, New York 11788-3619
Tele. 631-231-7269   Fax 631-231-8175
e-mail: Novascience@earthlink.net
Web Site: http://www.novapublishers.com

All rights reserved. No part of this book may be reproduced, stored in a retrieval system or transmitted in any form or by any means: electronic, electrostatic, magnetic, tape, mechanical photocopying, recording or otherwise without permission from the publishers.

The authors and publisher have taken care in preparation of this book, but make no expressed or implied warranty of any kind and assume no responsibility for any errors or omissions. No liability is assumed for incidental or consequential damages in connection with or arising out of information contained in this book.

This publication is designed to provide accurate and authoritative information with regard to the subject matter covered herein. It is sold with the clear understanding that the publisher is not engaged in rendering legal or any other professional services. If legal or any other expert assistance is required, the services of a competent person should be sought. FROM A DECLARATION OF PARTICIPANTS JOINTLY ADOPTED BY A COMMITTEE OF THE AMERICAN BAR ASSOCIATION AND A COMMITTEE OF PUBLISHERS.

Printed in the United States of America

Contents

Preface		vii
Chapter 1	Introduction	1
Chapter 2	The Nuclear Nonproliferation Regime	13
Chapter 3	Chemical and Biological Weapons Proliferation Regime	35
Chapter 4	Missile Proliferation Control Regime	47
Chapter 5	Appendix A. Proliferation Control Regime Membership	59
Chapter 6	Appendix B. Additional Legislation and Executive Orders	61
Index		63

PREFACE

This book provides information on the background and current status of the regimes intended to limit the spread of nuclear, chemical, and biological weapons and missiles. Weapons of mass destruction (WMD), especially in the hands of radical states and terrorists, represent a major threat to U.S. national security interests. Multilateral regimes were established to restrict world trade in these goods and technologies and to monitor certain civil applications.

The nuclear nonproliferation regime encompasses several treaties, extensive multilateral and bilateral diplomatic agreements, multilateral organizations and domestic agencies, and the domestic laws of participating countries. The nuclear regime represents a near-universal international consensus opposing any further spread of nuclear weapons. Since the beginning of the nuclear age, U.S. leadership has played a decisive role in the development of the regime. The regime is being challenged from several directions, as demonstrated by the Indian and Pakistani nuclear detonations in 1998. Many observers believe the success of the nuclear nonproliferation regime should be a top priority and that its outcome will strongly influence the effectiveness of other regimes dedicated to controlling chemical and biological weapons and missiles.

Chapter 1

INTRODUCTION

The United States has historically led the international community in establishing regimes intended to limit the spread of nuclear, chemical, and biological weapons and missiles. The regimes and their member countries use cooperative and coercive measures in pursuit of nonproliferation and counterproliferation objectives. Multilateral agreements and organizations are supplemented by strong bilateral cooperation among key allies, unilateral political and economic actions, and recourse to military operations should they become necessary. Congress supports the nonproliferation regimes primarily by providing statutory authority and funding for U.S. participation, establishing policy, and mandating punitive actions to help enforce the international standards set by the regimes.

The term "regime" often refers to the entire array of international agreements, multilateral organizations, national laws, regulations, and policies to prevent the spread of dangerous weapons and technologies. The regime that has evolved to limit the spread of nuclear weapons is the most extensive, followed by those dealing with chemical and biological weapons, and then by the missile regime. The difficulty of producing nuclear weapons material (highly enriched uranium or plutonium) and great awareness of nuclear weapons' destructiveness together have been conducive to creating a complex regime with widespread agreement on the priority of nuclear nonproliferation. Chemical weapons are easier to make and rely on readily available precursors, and they are far less destructive. Less is known about biological weapons, but they also rely on widespread dual-use technology and efforts to build a more extensive control regime are more recent. Finally, there is no international consensus on the danger of missile proliferation to support a nonproliferation treaty or a binding regime with enforcement mechanisms.

A key aspect of all the regimes is their attempt to control exports of sensitive goods and technologies through supplier agreements. These are the Nuclear Suppliers Group and the Zangger Committee for nuclear technology, the Australia Group for chemical and biological weapons technology, and the Missile Technology Control Regime. In the last decade, these export control regimes have expanded their membership, expanded and refined their control lists, and increased coordination among member states. At the same time, however, the non-binding nature of some of the regimes and growing resistance to them by certain countries, including some regime members, limits their effectiveness. A major dilemma is whether to include new members such as Russia and China that are not U.S. allies and do not have reliable export controls, or to limit membership to countries with excellent nonproliferation credentials. Regime members are afforded special access to controlled technology by the other members, so this issue also affects decisions on whether to include non-allies. Table 1 lists the proliferation control regimes, their components and statutory authority. There are many arms control treaties and other activities that address aspects of WMD and conventional weapons beyond the regimes covered in this report.[1]

STATUS AND TRENDS

The nonproliferation regimes have prevented many risky transfers over the years. However, several factors undermine their effectiveness. One factor is the difficulty of addressing underlying motivations of countries to acquire weapons of mass destruction (WMD). Regional security conditions as well as the desire to compensate for other countries' superior conventional or unconventional forces have been common motivations for WMD programs. Some countries, such as Iraq, may want WMD to dominate their adversaries. Prestige is another reason why certain countries seek WMD. Another factor working against the regimes is the steady diffusion of technology over time - much of the most significant WMD technology is 50 years old, and growing access to dual-use equipment makes it easier for countries or groups to build their own WMD factories from commonly available civilian equipment.

---

[1] For coverage of these subjects, see CRS Report RL30033, Arms Control and Nonproliferation Activities: A Catalog of Recent Events, by Amy Woolf.

Multilateral nonproliferation efforts face many difficulties. In the nuclear nonproliferation regime, many non-weapons states link their continued cooperation with progress in U.S.-Russian arms control, which they view as part of the bargain of the Treaty on the Nonproliferation of Nuclear Weapons Treaty (NPT). Some of these countries see the U.S. Senate's rejection of the Comprehensive Test Ban Treaty as a U.S. rejection of its obligations under the NPT. Russia and China in the past have linked nonproliferation cooperation with their objections to U.S. policies on missile defenses, especially V.S. withdrawal from the Anti-Ballistic Missile (ABM) Treaty. Other countries link nonproliferation to regional politics. Egypt, for example, has linked its continued participation in the NPT to gaining Israeli and U.S. concessions in Middle East peace talks. Some countries want to loosen controls on exports to countries such as Iran, Iraq, Libya, and India. Domestically, certain U.S. industries have waged a successful battle against V.S. export controls, which have been reduced and streamlined. The U.S.. government in recent years has been sympathetic to many of these concerns and has tried to accommodate them. However, efforts to accommodate objections to nonproliferation policies may have undermined their effectiveness.

STATE-TO-STATE RELATIONS

In addition to a formal framework of control agreements, close political relationships with key allies and other countries are very important for U.S. efforts to counter the spread and the use of WMD. International cooperation has been essential in extending the Nuclear Non-Proliferation Treaty, approving the Chemical Weapons Convention, building a broad consensus against nuclear tests, eliminating the nuclear weapons of Belarus, Kazakhstan, and Ukraine, and restraining proliferation in Iraq, Iran and North Korea. Initiatives by allies, such as the G-8 Global Partnership to combat the spread of WMD, demonstrate resolve to tackle specific proliferation problems. Many of these relationships, nonetheless, are strongly influenced by other political, military, and economic issues that sometimes take precedence over proliferation concerns. In practice, nonproliferation competes with important policy objectives such as trade, regional issues, and domestic political considerations, and there are often tensions and inconsistencies between nonproliferation and other policy objectives. Since September 11th, awareness of the inherent dangers that are posed by potential terrorist access to weapons of mass destruction has grown. In an article in July 2002, Assistant Secretary of State for Nonproliferation John S. Wolf called for all states to "elevate security against WMD and missile proliferation to an overarching imperative that trumps other, secondary considerations."[2] However, it is not clear what that "security against WMD proliferation" might entail and whether it encompasses the range of nonproliferation policies or just protection against imminent attacks.

A more difficult challenge exists when key U.S. allies and friends seek WMD and missiles of their own or transfer WMD technology. In that circumstance, a breakthrough in establishing trust and cooperation might ease some of the underlying security concerns that motivate countries to acquire WMD or to transfer WMD technology. Perhaps the hardest challenge for nonproliferation policies is to reduce the desire of countries for weapons of mass destruction. It is sometimes possible to change regional security conditions through alliances, arms transfers, arms control, or negotiations aimed at settling conflicts. However, eliminating underlying motivations takes time, and the next best option may be to delay WMD development for as long as possible.

Unilaterally, the United States uses sanctions to support its nonproliferation objectives. Various laws authorize or require the President to impose unilateral sanctions on countries that acquire, use, or help other countries to obtain WMD or missiles. Sanctions can affect U.S. aid, cooperation, and impose restrictions on U.S. technology exports. The effectiveness of sanctions often depends on persuading other countries to support or respect U.S. sanctions. Even without multilateral support, sanctions can still highlight strong U.S. opposition to WMD proliferation. However, strong sanctions are rarely imposed on U.S. friends or allies that acquire WMD.

COUNTERPROLIFERATION, INTELLIGENCE, AND DETERRENCE

Because most potential adversaries currently have WMD and missile delivery systems, and because diplomacy may fail to prevent further WMD proliferation, the U.S. armed forces have developed programs to help prevent the spread of WMD, to deter or prevent their use, and to protect against their effects. Defense cooperation and arms transfers to U.S. allies

---

[2] [http://usinfo.state.gov/journals/itps/0702/ijpe/ijpe0702.htm].

can ease concerns about security that can lead them to consider acquiring WMD, and also signal potential adversaries that acquisition or use of WMD may evoke a strong military response. U.S. conventional and nuclear military capabilities and the threat of retaliation help deter WMD attacks against U.S. forces, territory, or allies. Counterproliferation capabilities have been expanded in recent years to include more advanced "passive" and "active" defense measures. Passive counterproliferation tools include protective gear such as gas masks and detectors to warn of the presence of WMD. Active measures include missile defenses to protect U.S. territory, forces, and allies; precision-guided penetrating munitions and special operation forces to attack WMD installations; and intelligence gathering and processing capabilities. Intelligence is a particularly critical element of U.S. nonproliferation efforts, without which many policy options would not be possible. Intelligence agencies track foreign WMD programs, monitor treaty compliance, and attempt to detect transfers of WMD goods and technology. The U.S. cooperates with certain allies to prepare for possible counterproliferation actions. Although U.S. forces successfully attacked some WMD facilities in Iraq during the Gulf War, political and technical hurdles (hidden underground bunkers, locations near civilians, etc.) make counterproliferation a last resort if other options have failed.

CONGRESSIONAL ROLE

Congress has been actively engaged in nonproliferation legislation for close to sixty years. In addition to laws affecting diplomacy, treaty implementation and military options, legislation effecting restrictions on foreign aid, sanctions and export controls help establish nonproliferation policy and congressional oversight of executive branch nonproliferation policies.

Congress enacted strict controls on nuclear energy and cooperation in the first Atomic Energy Act of 1946. By the 1950s, however, it became clear that the U.S. nuclear weapons program needed materials from abroad and that pure denial of materials and technology had neither stopped the Soviet Union nor the UK from acquiring nuclear weapons. The 1954 revision of the Atomic Energy Act reflected a shift in strategy from that of prevention through denial to one of "influence through cooperation."[3] However, as allies planned to sell sensitive enrichment and reprocessing equipment to

---

[3] CRS Report 83-119, *Evolution or U.S. Nuclear Export Controls*, p. 7.

states outside of the NPT in the 1970s (e.g., Pakistan, South Korea, and Brazil), Congress reacted by passing several laws to slow down nuclear commerce and implement sanctions against those states clandestinely pursuing nuclear weapons. Controls on exports of chemical and biological agents with military applications and missiles have been regulated under the Arms Export Control Act (AECA) of 1968, and their dual-use technologies have been regulated under the Export Administration Act (EAA) of 1979 and its predecessors, but these controls were implemented relatively later in the *1980s*. Table 2 lists the major U.S. laws enacted to limit the transfer of WMD and WMD technology. Over time, most laws have been amended to address the range of WMD threats, but there are a few laws that address only one kind of weapon of mass destruction; some laws have focused on a proliferation threat from a particular country. Nunn-Lugar-related legislation and the Freedom Support Act address the range of WMD, but focus on Russia and the NIS. In addition, legislation related to Iraq and Iran span the range of WMD proliferation. See Appendix B for relevant text from nonproliferation-related legislation.

ORGANIZATION OF THE BOOK

The following sections will describe the nuclear, biological, chemical, and missile nonproliferation regimes. Each section will include: (a) a background section with a brief history of the regime; (b) a section setting out the treaties and agreements that authorize or affect the regime; (c) a brief description of how the regime is implemented; (d) U.S. laws authorizing or affecting the regime; and (e) issues for 107th Congress. More detailed information on regime membership, specific provisions in law and relevant executive orders are contained in appendices.

Table 1. Proliferation Control Regimes

Regime	Formal Treaties	Suppliers Groups and Informal Agreements	International Organization	U.S. Statutory Basis	U.S. Government Agencies Active
Nuclear	Nuclear Nonproliferation Treaty (NPT), 1970 Convention on Physical Protection of Nuclear Material, 1987 Treaty of Tlatelolco Treaty of Rarotonga Treaty of Pelindaba Treaty of Bangkok START Protocols Treaty of Moscow, 2002	Zangger Committee, 1971 Nuclear Suppliers' Group 1975 G-8	IAEA UN Conference on Disarmament	AEA, 1954 NNPA, 1978 FAA, 1961 AECA, 1976 EAA, 1979 NPPA, 1994 Ex-Im Bank, 1945 Nunn-Lugar, 1991 Iran-Iraq Arms Nonpro Act, 1992 Iran Nonpro Act, 2000	State, Defense, Commerce, Energy (+ national laboratories), Treasury, NRC, intelligence agencies
Chemical and Biological	Geneva Protocol, 1925 Chemical Weapons (CWC) 1993 Convention Biological and Toxin Weapons Convention (BWC)	Australia Group, 1984	OPCW UN Conference on Disarmament	EAA, 1979 AECA, 1976 Biological Weapons Anti-Terrorism Act Chem-Bio Weapons Control Warfare Elim Act, 1991 Nunn-Lugar Freedom Support Act Iran-Iraq Arms NP Act, 1992 Iran NP Act, 2000	State, Defense, Commerce, Treasury, intelligence agencies

Regime	Formal Treaties	Suppliers Groups and Informal Agreements	International Organization	U.S. Statutory Basis	U.S. Government Agencies Active
Missiles		Missile Technology Control Regime, 1987 International Code of Conduct, 2002		FAA, 1961 AECA, 1976 EAA, 1979 Missile Tech Control Act, 1990 Freedom Support Act Iran-Iraq NP Act	State, Defense, Commerce, Treasury, NASA, intelligence agencies

Table 2. U.S. Legal Framework for Proliferation Control

Title	Public Law	Application	Nuclear	Chemical	Biological	Missiles	Target Country	Notes
Export-Import Bank Act of 1945	P.L. 79-173 P.L. 107-189 reauth	Financing cutoff	X	X	X	X	Various	P.L. 107-189 added enforcement of AECA, EAA, IEEPA as justification for denying financing, extending purview of law to CW/ BW/missile areas
Atomic Energy Act 1954	P.L. 83-703	Exports; cutoff	X Sec 129				Various	P.L. 95-242 added Sec 129
Foreign Assistance Act 1961	P.L. 87-195	Aid cutoff	X Sec 307e	X	X	X Sec 498 A(b)	Various Russia	NPPA repealed relevant sections in FAA and placed them in AECE. Reference to FAA is deemed now to refer to section 101 or 102 in AECA.
Arms Export Control Act 1968	P.L. 90-629	Exports, aid cutoff; sanctions	X Sec 3f Sec101, 102*	X Sec 81**	X Sec 81	X Sec 72. 73, 74	Various	*NPPA 94 **P.L. 102-182 91
Nuclear Non-Proliferation Act 1978	P.L. 95-242	Sanctions	X				Various	
Export Administration Act 1979	P.L. 96-72	Export controls	X Sec 5,6	X Sec 6m, 11C	X Sec 6m, 11C	X Sec 5, 61, 11B	Various	Sec 11C added in 1991 by P.L. 102-182.

Title	Public Law	Application	Nuclear	Chemical	Biological	Missiles	Target Country	Notes
Biological Anti-Terrorism Act 1989	P.L. 101-298	Treaty; BWC			X		N.A.	Implements BWC
Missile Technology Control Act 1990	P.L. 101-510, Title XVII	Sanctions				X	Various	Added Chapter VII to AECA, Sections 6(1) and 11b to EAA 1979
Chemical and Biological Weapons Control and Warfare Elimination Act 1991*	P.L. 102-182, Title III	Sanctions		X	X		Various	
Nunn-Lugar 1991 Cooperative Threat Reduction Act 1993	P.L. 102-228 P.L. 103-160	Assistance programs	X X	X X	X X	X X	Russia	Amendment to CFE Treaty: Title XI
Iran-Iraq Nonproliferation Act 1992	P.L. 102-484 Title XVI	Sanctions	X	X	X	X	Iran, Iraq	
Freedom Support Act	P.L. 102-511 Title V	Assistance programs	X	X	X	X	NIS	
Nuclear Proliferation Prevention Act 1994	P.L. 103-236, Title VIII	Sanctions	X				Various	Consolidated np legislation into AECE, moving it from FAA
Chemical Weapons Convention Implementation Act 1998	P.L. 105-277	Treaty: CWC		X			N.A.	

Title	Public Law	Application	Nuclear	Chemical	Biological	Missiles	Target Country	Notes
Iran Nonproliferation Act 2000	P.L. 106-178	Sanctions	X	X	X	X	Iran	
Kenneth M. Ludden Foreign Operations, Export Financing-Related Program Appropriations Act, 2002	P.L. 107-115	Financing, assistance cutoff	X				Russia-Iran	No provision for presidential waiver

Chapter 2

THE NUCLEAR NONPROLIFERATION REGIME[4]

The nuclear nonproliferation regime encompasses several major treaties, extensive multilateral and bilateral diplomatic agreements, multilateral organizations and domestic agencies, and the domestic laws of participating countries. The nuclear regime reflects near-universal international agreement to oppose any further spread of nuclear weapons. Since the beginning of the nuclear age, U.S. leadership has played a decisive role in the development of the regime. Many observers believe the success of the nuclear nonproliferation regime is necessary for the effectiveness of other regimes dedicated to controlling chemical and biological weapons and missiles. Thus, they believe that preserving the nuclear regime should be a top priority.

In 2002, there were five declared nuclear weapons states (United States, Russia, Great Britain, France, China), three *de facto* nuclear weapons states (India, Israel, Pakistan), and one country - North Korea - that has probably secretly produced enough plutonium for one or two bombs. This is considerably less than predicted 40 years ago, when President Kennedy warned of the possibility that, by the 1970s, the United States could "face a world in which fifteen or twenty or twenty-five nations may have these weapons."

The nonproliferation regime has not stopped all proliferation, but it has helped restrain nuclear ambitions and solidified an international norm of behavior strongly condemning proliferation. Many countries that could make

---

[4] Prepared by Carl E. Behrens, Specialist in Energy Policy, Resources, Science, and Industry Division.

nuclear weapons have not, but some have at one time or another taken significant steps towards acquiring a nuclear weapons capability. Argentina, Brazil, South Africa, Iran, Iraq, Libya, North Korea, Taiwan, Sweden, and South Korea all have had nuclear weapons development programs. Both Japan and Germany had nuclear weapons programs during the Second World War, but did not succeed in making nuclear weapons before their programs were halted at the end of the war. Argentina, Brazil, South Korea, Sweden, Taiwan, and South Africa abandoned their nuclear weapons programs and joined the NPT as non-nuclear-weapon-states. Ukraine, Kazakhstan, and Belarus, as former Soviet republics with inherited nuclear weapons on their soil, also opted to join the NPT as non-nuclear-weapon-states.

Only a few countries maintain an interest in developing nuclear weapons, but it is difficult to predict how many countries or terrorist groups may in the future want a nuclear weapons capability. Some of the major challenges in preventing proliferation will include:

- controlling nuclear materials smuggling from the former Soviet Union and other countries with weak controls, a task of greater priority following the terrorist attacks of September 11th;
- strengthening physical protection of all source and special nuclear materials globally;
- strengthening the International Atomic Energy Agency's safeguards system;
- implementing the Agreed Framework and enforcing NPT obligations in North Korea;
- restraining nuclear proliferation in India and Pakistan;
- restraining nuclear programs in the Middle East, including those of Israel, Iran and Iraq;
- preventing U.S. technology from aiding the development of WMD and delivery systems in foreign countries;
- strengthening international verification and enforcement of nonproliferation agreements.

TREATIES AND AGREEMENTS

The NPT (http://www.iaea.org/worldatom/Documents/Legal/npttext.shtml] is the centerpiece of nonproliferation efforts. Other relevant treaties include regional nuclear-weapon-free zones and the Convention on the Physical Protection of Nuclear Material. In addition to these multilateral treaties, the United States has also entered into bilateral agreements and initiatives, such as the G-8 Global Partnership to Combat WMD. Finally, actions the United States takes in related areas of arms control may have an impact on the nonproliferation regime.

Treaty on the Nonproliferation of Nuclear Weapons (NPT), 1970

It took just three months after the bombing of Hiroshima and Nagasaki in 1945 for the first proposals to emerge from governments to control the "destructive uses" of nuclear energy. It took twenty-five years, however, for the NPT to emerge as the blueprint for nuclear nonproliferation.[5] In 1968, the treaty demarcated nuclear-weapon-states from non-nuclear-weapon-states by defining nuclear-weapon-states as those states that have manufactured and exploded a nuclear weapon or other nuclear explosive device prior to January 1, 1967. This definition implied that there would only ever be five "legitimate" nuclear-weapon-states — the United States, Russia, Great Britain, France, and China. All other states would join as non-nuclear weapon-states, agreeing not to acquire nuclear weapons in exchange for assistance in the peaceful uses of nuclear energy. In 2002, there were 187 parties to the NPT, including all five nuclear weapons states. The NPT completed its 25-year initial life-span in 1995, at which time members voted to make the treaty permanent.

The pledge not to acquire nuclear weapons is verified through the application of "nuclear safeguards" measures. The International Atomic Energy Agency (IAEA), founded in 1957, devised a system of nuclear material accountancy coupled with periodic and special inspections to ensure that nuclear material is not diverted from peaceful uses to military uses. Each non-nuclear-weapon-state party to the NPT must negotiate an agreement with the IABA to submit all nuclear material in its possession to regular inspections.[6] After learning several lessons from Iraq's and North Korea's

---

[5] Previous proposals included a 1945 proposal by the United States, Britain, and Canada proposed to establish a U.N. Atomic Energy Commission to eliminate "the use of atomic energy for destructive purposes," a 1957 "package" of measures (from Canada, UK, France, and United States) to the U.N. Disarmament Commission that included a commitment not to transfer nuclear weapons, and a 1964 program proposed by the United States for nonproliferation. See *Arms Control and Disarmament Agreements: Texts and Histories of the Negotiations,* 1990 edition, U.S. Arms Control and Disarmament Agency, p. 89.

[6] These agreements are called "full-scope safeguards." Other states have partial safeguards agreements, including India, Pakistan and, Israel, which can either apply to material or

clandestine nuclear programs, the IAEA launched a major effort to strengthen its safeguards system (see below) in 1992.

The incentive for non-nuclear-weapon-states to submit to inspections is a promise by advanced nuclear countries to promote "the fullest possible exchange of equipment, materials and scientific and technological information for the peaceful uses of nuclear energy."[7] The nuclear-weapon-states also agree to "pursue negotiations in good faith on effective measures relating to cessation of the nuclear arms race at an early date and to nuclear disarmament."[8]

In 1995, NPT members (now numbering 187) voted to make the treaty permanent like many other treaties. The members also agreed on a stronger review process to oversee compliance with the treaty. However, many members of the NPT are dissatisfied and the future of the treaty is not guaranteed. (See discussion of implementation for more details.)

Convention on the Physical Protection of Nuclear Material, 1987

The Convention on the Physical Protection of Nuclear Material [http://www.iaea.org/worldatom/Documents/Infcircs/Others/inf274rl.shtml] sets international standards for nuclear trade and commerce. The treaty had 77 parties in 2002. The Convention outlines security requirements for the protection of nuclear materials against terrorism and provides for the prosecution and punishment of offenders of international nuclear trade laws. Parties to the treaty agree to report to the IAEA on the disposition of nuclear materials being transported and agree to provide appropriate security during such transport.

For several years, the United States has been trying to strengthen this treaty to address the issue of nuclear terrorism by extending controls to domestic facility security, not just transportation. Amendments proposed thus far have included extending the Convention's scope to cover not only nuclear material in international transport, but also nuclear material in domestic use, storage, and transport, as well as the protection of nuclear material and facilities from sabotage.

---

facilities. All of the five nuclear weapon states have voluntary safeguards agreements, which cover a portion of facilities and materials.
[7] NPT, Article IV-2.
[8] NPT, Article VI.

Nuclear-Weapon-Free Zones

In the last 35 years, some states have concluded treaties to declare their regions to be "nuclear-weapons-free." These regions now include Latin America, the South Pacific, Africa, and Southeast Asia.

Treaty for the Prohibition of Nuclear Weapons in Latin America Treaty of Tlatelolco)[9]

This treaty establishes a nuclear-weapons free zone (NWFZ) in Latin America. Protocol I of the Treaty obligates non-Latin American countries that have territories in the zone (U.S., U.K., Netherlands, France) to accept the provisions of the treaty with respect to those territories. Protocol n contains a negative security pledge by the nuclear weapons states (China, France, Russia, U.K., U.S.) "not to use or threaten to use nuclear weapons against the Contracting Parties of the Treaty...." In 1994, Treaty holdouts Argentina, Brazil, and Chile signed on, and in 1995 Cuba signed the Treaty (but has not yet ratified it).

South Pacific Nuclear Free Zone (Treaty of Rarotonga)

[http://www.iaea.org/worldatom/lDocuments/Inicircs/Others/inf331.shtml] Eleven nations of the South Pacific have established a NWFZ for their region which prohibits the possession of nuclear weapons by its members and bans the manufacture or permanent emplacement of nuclear weapons within the zone by signatories outside of the Pacific region. The Treaty does not inhibit transit through the zone by nuclear-armed or powered military ships or aircraft. In 1996, the United States, France, and Britain signed the protocols to the Treaty, which are nearly identical to those of the Treaty of Tlatelolco. Before signing the treaty protocols, France conducted its last nuclear tests at its test site in French Polynesia. The United States is the only nuclear-weapon-state that has not ratified the protocol.

African Nuclear Weapon-Free-Zone Treaty (Treaty of Pelindaba)

[http://www.iaea.org/worldatom/Documents/Legal/pelindab.shtml] In April 1996, 53 countries signed the Treaty of Pelindaba, declaring Africa a NWFZ. The African NWFZ closely follows the models of the South Pacific and Latin American zones, and thus was able to attract the support of the United States and other weapons states after certain criteria were satisfied. This nuclear weapon-free-zone is not yet in force and the United States and Russia have not ratified the relevant protocol.

---

[9] [http://wwwiaea.orgiworldatom/Documents/Legal/bginf179.shtml]

Southeast Asia Nuclear Weapon-Free-Zone (Treaty of Bangkok)
[http://www.iaea.org/worldatom/Documents/Infcircs/1998/infcirc548.pdf] A group of 10 Southeast Asian nations declared a NWFZ for their region in late 1995 and the treaty entered into force in 1997. The United States and other weapons states declined to sign the protocols to the zone because the treaty contained controversial definitions of its members' sovereignty over territorial seas. The United States maintains that the language of the treaty is inconsistent with the Law of the Sea and could inflame territorial disputes as well as interfere with rights of passage. Modifications of the language are under consideration. In 1999, China announced it would sign the protocol but has deferred its signature.

Other Agreements

The United States has concluded arrangements with several states on a bilateral basis and on a multilateral basis in an effort to address specific programs. The most notable of these arrangements is the U.S.-North Korea Agreed Framework, but others include the recent "10 plus 10 over 10" effort within the G- 7 to provide additional funding for nuclear nonproliferation assistance to Russia and the newly independent states of the former Soviet Union (NIS).

The U.S.-North Korea Agreed Framework

In October 1994, the United States signed an agreement with North Korea to exchange its existing nuclear reactors and reprocessing equipment for modern light water reactor technology that is somewhat less suited to making bombs.[10] North Korea is also receiving shipments of heavy fuel oil to compensate for energy that theoretically might have been generated from the reactors it agreed to shut down. The deal requires North Korea to eventually resolve outstanding safeguards violations, including its

---

[10] North Korea joined the NPT in 1985, but delayed inspectionsunti11992. In February 1993, North Korea denied access by IAEA inspectors to two sites which IAEA (and U.S. intelligence) believed held evidence of clandestine nuclear work. On March 12, 1993, North Korea notified the United Nations Security Council that it was withdrawing from the NPT, which permits withdrawal after 3 months notice. It subsequently suspended its withdrawal, but claimed to have "unique status" under the NPT, and continued to block inspections. Estimates vary on the amount of plutonium that North Korea might have separated; most agree that there is enough for 1-2 bombs but an accurate estimate awaits more information on the reactor operating history. See CRS Issue Brief IB91141, *North Korea's Nuclear Weapons Program).*

undeclared plutonium, before completion of the new reactors. Many details of the deal are still being negotiated.

South Korea actually will build the reactors and pay for about 60-70 percent of the deal. Japan and other countries are to pay for the rest. The United States is paying for the oil shipments and has agreed to pay for and provide safe storage of the spent nuclear fuel rods that were removed (illegally) from a 25 MW reactor in 1993. An international consortium called the Korean Peninsula Energy Development Organization (KEDO) was established in March 1995 to coordinate the reactor construction project. KEDO has negotiated several agreements with North Korea on the legal, financial and territorial aspects of the project. However, negotiations on the construction of the reactors have periodically broken down due to tensions between the two Koreas.

A key issue for Congress is the implementation of the agreement and the extent of the U.S. contribution. Some Members oppose using U.S. funds, but most apparently are not prepared to block implementation of the agreement.

10 plus 10 over 10

At the summit held in June 2002 in Kananaskis, Canada, G-8 members agreed to a Global Partnership to halt the spread of weapons of mass destruction and related materials and technology. The G-8 members agreed to raise $20 billion over 10 years in nonproliferation assistance to Russia, of which the United States committed to providing $10B. Projects relating to disarmament, nonproliferation, counterterrorism and nuclear safety will focus initially on Russia, but the initiative will be open to other states as well.[11] Although this effort may not become as formalized as the Agreed Framework, it illustrates the willingness of states to create mechanisms to address specific nonproliferation problems.

Related Arms Control Agreements

Article VI of the NPT calls for an end to the arms race and progress toward disarmament. For many non-nuclear-weapon-states, Article VI embodies the *quid pro quo* of the NPT - while non-nuclear-weapon-states give up their right to develop nuclear weapons, nuclear-weapon-states agree to eventually disarm. In the 1990s, the Comprehensive Test Ban Treaty

---

[11] See Fact Sheet on G-8 Summit: Preventing the Proliferation of Weapons of Mass Destruction, June 27, 2002, Office of the Press Secretary, The White House. [http://usinfo.state.gov]

(CTBT) was seen as the next step toward nuclear disarmament.[12] By the mid-1990s, all nuclear weapon states were observing a moratorium on testing, which the treaty would have made permanent. The parties completed negotiations and signed the CTBT in 1996; President Clinton submitted the treaty to the Senate in September 1997 and in 1999, the Senate refused to give its advice and consent.[13] Despite this action, U.S. delegates to the NPT review conference in 2000 reaffirmed the commitment to negotiate total nuclear disarmament.

Unilateral and bilateral reductions of nuclear weapons have also been important within the context of the nuclear nonproliferation regime as demonstrations of good faith by the nuclear weapon states towards the eventual goal of disarmament. In January 2002, the Bush Administration released the results of its "Nuclear Posture Review," announcing that U.S. nuclear planning would no longer address the "Russian threat," but would need to meet a range of threats from unspecified countries. The redirection would be accompanied by a large, unilateral reduction in deployed nuclear weapons. However, the new policy also included development of a controversial missile defense capability, improving the nuclear weapons "infrastructure" to allow resumption of testing, and possible development of new weapons more rapidly. Although the Administration statement did not indicate that such activities were contemplated or necessary, the suggestion that they might be in the future caused dismay in nonproliferation circles.[14] In May 2002, Presidents Bush and Putin signed what has become known as the Treaty of Moscow, which will reduce the number of deployed strategic nuclear weapons to between 1700 and 2200 by 2012.[15] This treaty has been viewed alternately by some observers as a step toward nuclear disarmament and by others as a step back from nuclear disarmament, since its reductions are not permanent and apply only to deployed forces rather than the stockpile of weapons as a whole.

Finally, for many countries, the ABM Treaty was an important symbol of a commitment by the United States and USSR to ratchet down the nuclear arms race, and its June 2002 abrogation represents to some a setback in disarmament. On the other hand, some observers have argued that U.S.

---

[12] In the early 1990s, a test ban and a treaty halting the production of nuclear material (known as fissile material production cutoff treaty), were viewed as the next steps. No progress has been made to date on negotiating a production cutoff treaty in the Conference on Disarmament.
[13] CRS Issue Brief IB92099, Nuclear Weapons: Comprehensive Test Ban Treaty.
[14] See CRS Report RS21133, The Nuclear Posture Review: Overview and Emerging Issues.
[15] See CRS Report RL31448, Nuclear Arms Control: the Strategy Offensive Reductions Treaty.

withdrawal from the treaty will have little impact on other states' nuclear force postures, including that of China.[16]

IMPLEMENTING THE REGIME

Although the Nuclear Nonproliferation Treaty (NPT) is perhaps the most visible aspect of the nuclear nonproliferation regime, the success of nonproliferation efforts relies on the sturdy functioning of national export control laws and implementation, the Zangger Committee and Nuclear Suppliers' Group multilateral coordination of export controls, and effective inspections conducted by the International Atomic Energy Agency (IAEA). Equally important is the *quid pro quo* of technical assistance in the peaceful uses of nuclear energy that the IAEA provides.

The International Atomic Energy Agency (IAEA)

The IAEA, a U.N.-affiliated international organization, was established in 1957 to "accelerate and enlarge the contribution of atomic energy to peace, health and prosperity," and to ensure "that assistance provided by it . . . is not used in such a way as to further any military purpose."[17] With the entry into force of the NPT in 1970, it performs the dual missions of verifying NPT obligations and providing assistance in peaceful nuclear technology to developing nations. By 2002, the Agency had 131 member states and an annual budget of about $225 million. The IAEA safeguards system monitors nuclear materials and technology to deter and detect diversions from peaceful to military uses.

The administrative structure of the Agency resembles that of the United Nations. The General Conference includes all members and meets annually. The Board of Governors has 35 members, nine of which are permanent advanced nuclear nations, with the remaining Board members serving one-year terms as representatives of regional nuclear interests. The Secretariat is the administrative arm of the Agency. It is headed by the Director General, who is the chief policy-making official. The current Director General, Dr. Mohamed El Baradei, is an Egyptian diplomat who previously served as head of the IAEA's legal department.

---

[16] *See* CRS Report RL 30699, Nuclear, Biologica4 and Chemical Weapons andMissiles: The Current Situation and Trends
[17] The IAEA Statute is found at: [http://www.iaea.org/worldatom/Documents/statute.html]

In more than 25 years of inspections, Iraq was the first country to be declared in violation of its IAEA safeguards agreement in 1991, followed just a few years later by North Korea. These declarations, and the experience of accounting for past nuclear activities in Iraq, South Africa, and throughout the former Soviet Union, galvanized the world community to agree to strengthen the IAEA's inspection/safeguards system. The IAEA developed a strengthened safeguards program (formerly called "93+2") to improve its ability to detect unreported nuclear activities in non-weapon states. The program includes:

- provision of intelligence information to the IABA by member states about suspect nuclear activities;
- access for inspectors to any location on a timely basis;
- new safeguards technology;
- measures to promote complete transparency and reporting *of* all nuclear commerce.
- sufficient financial resources to carry out the IAEA's expanded responsibilities.

State parties to the NPT have been required to ratify new "model protocol" agreements to their existing nuclear safeguards agreements with the IAEA. On May 9,2002, President Bush submitted the U.S. model protocol agreement to the Senate for its consent to ratification. Ratification, according to some observers, may present the United States with a stronger negotiating hand in persuading key states to accept the protocol. A continuing issue will be adequate funding for the IAEA safeguards. The annual $82M safeguards budget is insufficient to carry out the IAEA's new responsibilities; the Agency estimates it typically spends about $95M each year on safeguards, relying on extra-budgetary contributions. Thus, the IAEA's ability to carry out its growing responsibilities and efforts to upgrade its safeguards system continue to be limited by members' reluctance to increase the IAEA budget.

Since September 11th, the IAEA has been promoting efforts to help prevent terrorists from acquiring or using weapons of mass destruction, including nuclear or radiological devices. These have focused primarily on upgrading its assistance in physical security, in locating orphaned radioactive sources, and in promoting discussion of ways to enhance the Convention on the Protection of Physical Security. The IAEA established a Code of Conduct on the Safety and Security of Radioactive Sources in 2001 and an Action Plan on Combating Nuclear Terrorism in 2002.

The Zangger Committee

In 1971, a group of seven NPT nuclear supplier nations formed the Nuclear Exporters Committee, known as the Zangger Committee, to assist in restricting nuclear trade as called for in Article III the NPT. In 1974, the Zangger Committee compiled a list of nuclear export items that could be potentially useful for military applications of nuclear technology. The nuclear suppliers agreed that the transfer of items on the list would "trigger" a requirement for IAEA safeguards to assure that the items were not used to make nuclear explosives. The Zangger list included reactors, reactor components, and certain nuclear materials such as heavy water. In recent years, the list of controlled items has been expanded and updated. Membership is voluntary and implies no formal commitments for enforcement of the guidelines. By 2002, the Zangger Committee had 33 members[18] and continued to meet twice each year to exchange information and upgrade its list of controlled commodities.

The Nuclear Suppliers Group (NSG)

Shaken by the 1974 test of a nuclear explosive device by India, the major nuclear suppliers in 1975 established a set of unpublished nuclear export guidelines. In 1978, the group, known as the London Club, added new members and announced a common policy regarding nuclear exports. While the NPT's Zangger list initially included only nuclear materials and components used directly in weapons development, the London Club adopted more restrictive export control guidelines that included some dual-use items, with civil and military applications. The NSG guidelines called for suppliers to exercise restraint regarding transfers of enrichment and reprocessing technology, and required the provision of physical security for transferred nuclear facilities and materials, acceptance of safeguards on replicated facilities (based on a design transferred from a London Club member-state), and prohibitions against retransfer of nuclear exports to third parties.

Although NSG guidelines were in place, members took no further actions until 1991. Concerned about Iraq's successful procurement of dual-use items and apparently inconsistent enforcement of nuclear export controls in several supplier countries, the NSG convened in March 1991 for the first

---

[18] See Appendix A for list of Zangger Committee members.

time since 1978 to update its list of controlled commodities. The expanded group agreed on new guidelines in January 1992 for transfers of a wider range of nuclear-related, dual-use equipment, material and technology and jointly adopted the longstanding U.S. policy of requiring full-scope safeguards for all nuclear exports. (Nations purchasing nuclear technology must open all nuclear facilities to inspection, not just the facility in which an imported item is used).[19] By 2002, the NSG had expanded to 38 members.[20]

Some developing nations have objected to the work of the NSG because it further divides the technologically advanced nuclear "haves" from the "have nots" and creates additional obstacles to their access to nuclear technology. A few countries have turned to suppliers outside of the NSG (e.g., China) to avoid the requirement for full-scope safeguards on nuclear exports. The emergence of new nuclear suppliers that do not subscribe to NSG guidelines undermines the efforts of NSG members to control the spread of nuclear weapons.

The strengthening of NSG export policy after the Gulf War responded to numerous examples of illegal, covert, and suspicious nuclear trade involving Western firms and countries such as India, Iraq, Iran, Israel, Pakistan, Brazil, Argentina, South Africa, and others. These transfers underscored the limitations of voluntary export controls, but they also motivated U.S. officials to push for further tightening of NSG restrictions on world nuclear exports. However, as a voluntary association, the NSG has no formal administrative structure, no legal authority to influence the nuclear trade policies of its members, and no formal enforcement mechanism.

U.S. Government Organization

The Departments of State, Energy, Defense, Commerce and the intelligence community are all involved in the formulation and implementation of nonproliferation policy.

- The National Security Council coordinates nonproliferation policy.
- The State Department, in consultation with the Energy Department, negotiates U.S. agreements for nuclear cooperation and represents U.S. nonproliferation interests with other states and international organizations such as the IAEA.

---

[19] The new guidelines appeared as an International Atomic Energy Agency document, INFCIRC/254/Rev.1/Part 1 and Part 2, July 1992.
[20] See Appendix A for NSG membership.

- The Department of Defense is responsible for counterproliferation strategy and policy, and also administers Cooperative Threat Reduction programs in the former Soviet Union.
- The Department of Energy provides expertise in nuclear weapons to support nonproliferation policy and diplomacy, largely through its national laboratories. DOE also administers nonproliferation programs to control fissile material in the former Soviet Union.
- The Nuclear Regulatory Commission licenses nuclear exports subject to concurrence by the Department of State.
- The Department of Commerce oversees licensing of dual-use exports as mandated by Section 309(c) of the Nuclear Non-Proliferation Act, which requires controls on "all export items, other than those licensed by the NRC, which could be, if used for purposes other than those for which the export is intended, of significance for nuclear explosive purposes."
- The Department of the Treasury oversees U.S. embargoes through its Office of Foreign Assets Control, and enforces export control through the U.S. Customs Service;
- The CIA has a Nonproliferation Center that coordinates intelligence aspects of nonproliferation policy.
- Several interagency working groups coordinate the various responsibilities for nonproliferation policy.

Since September 11th, significant U.S. government interest has focused on counterproliferation programs - that is, military measures against weapons of mass destruction. Although the Department of Defense has had programs in place for several years, efforts in this area have been renewed. Counterproliferation includes active and passive defenses to protect U.S. and allied troops, although protection against nuclear weapons is far more difficult than protecting against chemical weapons. Since September 11th, public attention has been drawn to the possibility of preemptive strikes on WMD capabilities, particularly in the case of Iraq. The Bush Administration, however, has not yet attempted to make a clear and comprehensive case for such action to the U.S. public. The implications for the nonproliferation regime, which could be significant, are unclear.

U.S. Laws[21]

The main legislative pillars of U.S. nuclear nonproliferation policy are the Atomic Energy Act of 1954, the Nuclear Non-Proliferation Act of 1978, and the Foreign Assistance Act 1961/Arms Export Control Act 1968.

The Atomic Energy Act of 1954 (AEA)[22]

The Atomic Energy Act of 1954 established legal authority for the commercial and military development of nuclear energy. It gave primary authority for the development and oversight of the U.S. government's nuclear programs to a civilian agency: the Atomic Energy Commission (now the Nuclear Regulatory Commission). In 1974, these duties were divided between the NRC and the Department of Energy. A major purpose of the Act was to establish controls on the export of nuclear materials, goods, information, and technology. Under the ABA, the State Department must negotiate an agreement for nuclear cooperation as a precondition for exports of sensitive U.S. nuclear technology to any foreign country. Each agreement must meet several standards outlined in the ABA. Moreover, the Act contains penalties and restrictions for countries that do not uphold the terms of nuclear agreements with the United States. Congress reviews all such agreements before they can enter into force.

The Nuclear Non-Proliferation Act of 1978 (NNPA)[23]

Congress and the Carter Administration viewed U.S. leadership and control over the international nuclear fuel cycle as an. effective means of restraining the spread of uranium enrichment and plutonium reprocessing facilities throughout the world. Enrichment and reprocessing technologies are key technologies for states aspiring to develop nuclear weapons. While reaffirming the U.S. commitment to be a reliable supplier of nuclear technology and fuels, the Act established an important new requirement for nations importing U.S. nuclear technology and materials: they must accept full-scope safeguards on their entire nuclear program. This standard was

---

[21] This section drawn from CRS Report RL31502,Nuclear, Biological, Chemical and Missile Proliferation Sanctions: Selected Current Law.
[22] P.L. 83-703, 42 U.S.C. 2011.
[23] P.L. 95-242, 22 U.S.C. 3201.

adopted by NSG members in 1992. The Act also established a requirement of prior U.S. approval for retransfers or reprocessing of material or equipment as well as to material produced using U.S.-exported technology. These measures gave the United States much more control over the foreign uses of U.S.-origin nuclear material.

Title III of the NNPA includes such varied measures as requiring the Department of Energy to obtain NRC licenses to distribute source and special material and establishment of criteria for terminating nuclear exports from the United States (which affects bilateral nuclear cooperation agreements) to include detonation of a nuclear device, termination/abrogation or violation of IAEA safeguards, or engaging in activities involving nuclear material which have significance in the manufacture of nuclear explosive devices (covering a wide array of activities). Additional prohibited acts included violating a nuclear cooperation agreement with the United States; assisting a non-nuclear-weapon-state in activities involving nuclear material that could potentially help in the manufacture or acquisition of a nuclear explosive device; or enriching any U.S. source or special material without the permission of the United States. The NNPA requires (in Section 601) the President to report annually to the Congress on the Government's efforts to prevent nuclear proliferation.

Foreign Assistance Act/Arms Export Control Act (AECA)[24]

The Arms Export Control Act (AECA), as amended, authorizes U.S. Government military sales, loans, leases, financing, and licensing of commercial arms sales to other countries. The AECA coordinates such actions with other foreign policy considerations, including nonproliferation, and determines eligibility of recipients for military exports, sales, leases, loans, and financing.

- *Section 3(f) (22 U.S.C. 2753(f))* prohibits U.S. military sales or leases to any country that the President determines is in material breach of binding commitments to the United States under international treaties or agreements regarding nonproliferation of

---

[24] P.L. 90-629, 22 U.S.C. 2751. Title 22 of the U.S. Code, Chapter 39, addresses Arms Export Control. Subchapter VII addresses control of missiles and missile exports or technology; subchapter VIII addresses chemical weapons and biological weapons, and subchapter X addresses nuclear nonproliferation controls.

nuclear explosive devices and unsafeguarded special nuclear material.

- *Section 40 (22 U.S.C. 2780)* prohibits exports or assistance in exporting (financial or otherwise) munitions to countries that provide support for terrorism. Included in the definition of acts of international terrorism are: "all activities that the Secretary [of State] determines willfully aid or abet the international proliferation of nuclear explosive devices to individuals or groups or willfully aid or abet an individual or groups in acquiring unsafeguarded special nuclear material." The President can rescind a determination or waive sanctions if essential to the national security interests of the United States.

- *Section 101 (22 U.S.C. 2799aa)* (formerly section 669 of the FAA) prohibits foreign economic or military assistance to countries that deliver or receive nuclear enrichment equipment, materials, or technology unless the supplier agrees to place such under safeguards and the recipient has full-scope safeguards. The President, who makes the determination, can waive sanctions if they will have a serious adverse effect on vital U.S. interests, given assurances that the recipient will not acquire, develop, or assist others in acquiring or developing nuclear weapons.

- *Section 102 (22 U.S. C. 2799aa-1)* (formerly section 670 of the FAA) prohibits foreign economic or military assistance to countries that deliver or receive nuclear reprocessing equipment, material, or technology to or from another country; or any non-nuclear-weapon-state which illegally exports from the United States items that would contribute to nuclear proliferation. The President, who makes the determination, can waive the sanction if he finds that ending assistance would adversely affect U.S. nonproliferation objectives or jeopardize the common defense and security. The section further prohibits assistance (except humanitarian or food assistance), defense sales, export licenses for U.S. Munitions List items, other export licenses subject to foreign policy controls, and various credits and loans to any country that the President has determined transfers a nuclear explosive device, design information, or component to a non-nuclear-weapon-state, or is a non-nuclear-weapon-state and receives a nuclear device, design information, or component, or detonates a nuclear explosive device.

Much of the language on nuclear nonproliferation controls that had been incorporated into the Foreign Assistance Act earlier (including the 1977 Glenn-Symington amendments on enrichment and reprocessing and the 1985 Pressler amendment related to Pakistan) were incorporated into the AECA in 1994 by the Nuclear Proliferation Prevention Act (see discussion below).

In the Senate-passed version of the Security Assistance Act of 2002 (HR 1646 BAS), Sec. 205 would amend section 40d of the AECA (22 USC 2780(d)) to include the transfer of chemical, biological and radiological agents in those activities considered to be acts of international terrorism.

Export Administration Act of 1979 (EAA)

The Export Administration Act of 1979 (P.L. 96-72) authorizes the executive branch to regulate private sector exports of particular goods and technology to other countries. Although the Act expired in 1994, its provisions have been continued under executive orders.[25] The EAA coordinates such actions with other foreign policy considerations, including nonproliferation, and determines eligibility of recipients for exports. *Section 5 (50 U.S.C. app. 2404)* authorizes the President to curtail or prohibit the export of any goods or services for national security reasons: to comply with other laws regarding a potential recipient country's political status or political stability, to cooperate with international agreements or understandings, or to protect militarily critical technologies. *Section 6 (50 U.S.C. app. 2405)* authorizes the President to curtail or prohibit the export of goods or services for foreign policy reasons. Within Section 6, for example, *Section 6(j)* establishes the State Department's list of countries found to be supporting acts of international terrorism, a list on which many other restrictions and prohibitions in law are based. The current Senate version of the bill to reauthorize the EAA, S. 149, would shift the current authority to impose export controls on items related to WMD proliferation from foreign

---

[25] Authority granted by the Export Administration Act terminated on August 20, 1994 but continued under executive orders and then extended to August 20, 2001 by the Export Administration Modification and Clarification Act of 2000 (P.L. 106-508). On August 17, 2001, President Bush issued Executive Order 13222 (66 FR 44025) extending the authorities of the BAA for one year, and on August 14, 2002, the President continued the authority of Executive Order 13222 for another year. See Vol. 38, No. 33, pg. 1383 *Federal Register,* August 16, 2002.

policy controls to national security controls. As such, controls could be lifted if the items met foreign availability and mass market criteria, irrespective of the foreign policy behavior of the recipient state. Some critics maintain that this switch in categories would make it harder for the President to impose unilateral controls.[26]

Export-Import Bank Act of 1945

The Export-Import Bank Act of 1945 (P.L. 79-173) establishes the Export-Import Bank of the United States and authorizes the Bank to finance and facilitate exports and imports and the exchange of commodities and services between the United States and foreign countries. Key nuclear-nonproliferation-related provisions were added in 1978. These include *Section2(b)(1)(B)* (12 *U.S.C. 635(b) (1) (B)*) and *Section 2 (b)* (4) (12 *U.S.C. 635(b)(4))*, which together allow the Bank to deny credit generally if that credit does not help advance U.S. nuclear proliferation policy, and specifically, if a person or country has a) violated, abrogated or terminated a nuclear safeguards agreements; b) violated a nuclear cooperation agreement with the United States; or c) aided or abetted a non- nuclear-weapon state to acquire a nuclear explosive device or to acquire unsafeguarded special nuclear material. There is a provision for presidential waiver. (See Appendix B for details).

The Export-Import Bank Act of 1945 was recently amended[27] to allow denial of Ex-Im Bank financing for violations of the Foreign Corrupt Practices Act, the Arms Export Control Act, the International Emergency Economic Powers Act or the Export Administration Act of 1979, extending its purview from strictly nuclear to CW, BW, and missile-related concerns.

Nuclear Proliferation Prevention Act of 1994

In 1994 Congress passed the Nuclear Proliferation Prevention Act, (NPP A, Title VIII, of the Foreign Relations Authorization Act, Fiscal Years 1994 and 1995, P.L. 103-236) which primarily strengthened penalties against persons who aid or abet the acquisition of nuclear weapons or unsafeguarded

---

[26] See CRS Reports *RL30169,ExportAdministration Act of* 1979 *Reauthorization* and CRS Report RL30689, *EAA: Controversy and Prospects,* for discussions of current legislation related to this Act.
[27] See The Export-Import Bank Reauthorization Act of 2002, P.L. 107-189.

nuclear weapons materials, or countries (non-nuclear- weapon-states) that obtain or explode nuclear devices. Sanctions include: cutoff of U.S. assistance, prohibition on involvement with U.S. government procurement, stringent licensing requirements for technology exports, and opposition to loans or credits from international financial institutions. These sanctions were imposed on India and Pakistan following their nuclear tests in May 1998, but were gradually relaxed. Legislation passed in the 106th Congress extended the President's authority to relax sanctions on India and Pakistan for a year, and the Senate passed a bill suspending sanctions on the two countries for five years. The FY2000 Department of Defense Appropriations bill (P.L. 106-79) extended the authority to suspend sanctions. Following the September 11th terrorist attacks, President Bush lifted all remaining sanctions on India and Pakistan in response to support of U.S. operations in Afghanistan.

The NPPA defined for the first time in U.S. law the term "nuclear explosive device." It defined "terrorism" as used in the AECA, to include activities that assist groups or individuals to acquire any nuclear explosive device. It included a sense of Congress that identified 24 measures to strengthen IABA safeguards, some of which have been implemented. Relevant sections include *Section 821 (22 U.S.C. 3201 note)*, which requires U.S. government procurement sanctions; *Section 823 (22 U.S.C. 3201 note)*, which requires U S. executive directors of international financial institutions to vote against finance that might promote nuclear proliferation; and *Section 824 (22 U.S.C. 3201 note)*, which takes aim at financial institutions and persons involved with financial institutions from assisting nuclear proliferation through the provision of financing. (See Appendix B for specific details.)

Nunn-Lugar/Cooperative Threat Reduction Program Legislation

In late 1991, Congress passed the Nunn-Lugar Amendment, which established programs to assist with the safe and secure storage and dismantlement of nuclear weapons in Russia and the Newly Independent States (NIS). These programs initially focused on the "loose nukes" problem, but have broadened their focus to address a variety of proliferation risks associated with weak political control over nuclear materials, equipment, and expertise, as well as CW, BW, and missiles. This effort has expanded to include the CTR program in DoD and nonproliferation programs in DoE and the State Department.[28]

Iran-Iraq Arms Nonproliferation Act of 1992

Section 1602 of the Defense Authorization for FY 1993 (Title XVI, P.L 102-484, as amended) extended existing sanctions on Iraq to Iran. The law states that it is the policy of the United States to oppose any transfer to Iran or Iraq that could contribute to either country's ability to acquire nuclear, chemical, biological, or advanced conventional weapons. *Section 1604* requires the President to impose sanctions against any person whom he has determined to be engaged in such transfers. *Section 1605* similarly addresses activities of foreign governments. The 104th Congress amended the law (by passage of section 1408(a), P.L. 104-106, National Defense Authorization Act for Fiscal Year 1996) to make it apply to transfers contributing to the development of weapons of mass destruction as well as advanced conventional weapons.

Iran Nonproliferation Act of 2000

The law (P.L. 106-178) imposes penalties on countries whose companies help Iran's efforts to acquire weapons of mass destruction and missile delivery systems. This law covers all WMD.

ISSUES FOR THE 107TH CONGRESS

Since September 11th, much of Congress' attention in the area of the nonproliferation of weapons of mass destruction has focused on how to mitigate the threat U.S. citizens face right now improving domestic preparedness against WMD terrorism and improving intelligence capabilities to detect evidence of proliferation-related activities. As Congress ponders the appropriate allocation of resources and organizational responsibilities, one criteria, according to some observers, should be the extent to which reorganizations would dilute or improve U.S. organization to combat proliferation. Above all, however, most sources agree that the U.S.

---

[28] See CRS Report 97-1027, *Nunn-Lugar Cooperative Threat Reduction Programs: Issues for Congress.*

The Nuclear Nonproliferation Regime

government should continue to address nuclear proliferation at the source securing nuclear materials in Russia and the NIS and halting information flows from WMD-knowledgeable scientists to countries of proliferation concern.

Other key nuclear nonproliferation issues for Congress include:

- implementing DoD's Cooperative Threat Reduction programs to improve controls on nuclear materials, equipment, and expertise in Russia and the NIS and possibly expanding these efforts to countries outside the NIS;
- monitoring the "Agreed Framework" between the United States and North Korea to end Pyongyang's nuclear weapons program;
- monitoring Iran's nuclear program, including Russian and Chinese nuclear exports and assistance;
- opposing the nuclear arms race between India and Pakistan and preventing
- those countries from exporting WMD technology;
- strengthening the IAEA safeguards system to enforce the NPT and maintaining the NPT;
- maintaining and expanding adherence to NSG nuclear export control standards;
- curbing dangerous Chinese and Russian nuclear exports.

Closer to home, Congress will need to consider how to dispose of tons of excess plutonium from dismantled Russian and U.S. warheads without increasing proliferation risks; and how U.S. arms control and defense cooperation (particularly missile defense cooperation) might affect proliferation risks.

Chapter 3

CHEMICAL AND BIOLOGICAL WEAPONS PROLIFERATION REGIME[29]

Prohibitions against the use of chemical weapons date back to the International Peace Conferences that met at the Hague in 1899 and 1907; these pre-World War I prohibitions were reaffirmed in the 1919 Versailles Treaty and further expanded in the 1925 Geneva Protocol. Although public horror at the nature of these weapons rivals that accorded to nuclear weapons, it has been much more difficult to constrain their proliferation and use. Considered to be "the poor man's nuclear bomb," they do not require as extensive an infrastructure as do nuclear weapons and the technologies are much more widely disseminated. In addition, there has been a weaker consensus on the need to control these weapons, in part because they are viewed as less destructive than nuclear weapons. The regimes that have grown up around these weapons, while not as extensive as the nuclear nonproliferation regime, include treaties, supplier agreements, and domestic laws.

TREATIES AND AGREEMENTS

The Chemical Weapons Convention (CWC) and the Biological and Toxin Weapons Convention (BWC) are the two primary treaties related to CBW proliferation. The United States is a State Party to both the BWC and the CWC.

---

[29] Prepared by Steven R. Bowman, Specialist in National Defense, Foreign Affairs, Defense, and Trade Division.

Chemical Weapons Convention (CWC)

Culminating 25 years of negotiations, the Chemical Weapons Convention opened for signature in January 1993.[30] The CWC entered into force on April 29, 1997, and there are currently 145 state parties, including the United States.[31]

For states party to the treaty, the CWC prohibits the development, production, stockpiling, transfer, and use of chemical weapons. The Convention mandates the destruction of chemical weapon arsenals within ten years of its coming into force. The CWC also restricts the international transfer of chemicals deemed useful in the production of chemical weapons, so-called "precursors." Most precursor chemicals are dual-use, with legitimate peaceful applications. The CWC establishes extensive lists or "schedules" of precursors whose production, use, and transfer must be reported to the CWC's Organization for the Prohibition of Chemical Weapons (OPCW). The schedules are designated in order of their potential usefulness in chemical warfare. Schedule I chemicals may be exported m to states parties (i.e., nations that have ratified the CWC). In accordance with treaty provisions, as of April 2000, the export of Schedule n chemicals to non-states parties became prohibited, and as of April 2002, the extension of the export restrictions to Schedule ill chemicals is under consideration.

Biological and Toxin Weapons Convention

The Biological Weapons Convention was concluded in 1972, with U.S. ratification and entry in force in 1975.[32] The BWC has 124 states parties.[33] The Convention bans the development, production, and stockpiling of biological agents or toxins "of types and in quantities that have no justification for peaceful purposes." The development, manufacture, and possession of BW weapons or delivery systems is also prohibited. States parties also agree not to transfer biological agents or toxins for any but peaceful purposes.

In 1969, the United States declared a unilateral end to its offensive BW program and suggested separating the BW issue from the chemical-biological arms control negotiations in Geneva. Negotiations on this

---

[30] [http://www.opcw.org/html/db/cwc/eng/cwc_frameset.html]
[31] [http://www.opcw.org/html/db/members_frameset.html]
[32] [http://www.fas.orginuke/control/bwc/text/bwc.htm]
[33] [http://opbw.org]

proposal took only three years to conclude primarily because no verification provisions were included in the Convention.

IMPLEMENTING THE REGIME

International Organizations

The CBW nonproliferation regime relies on the Australia Group and the Organization for the Prohibition of Chemical Weapons (OPCW), which was created by the CWC. There is no independent international organization to administer the Biological Weapons Convention. Data exchanges required by the BWC are carried out through the United Nations, with the State Department as the international point of contact within the U.S. government.

Australia Group (AG)

In 1984, United Nations investigators officially confirmed that chemical weapons had been used in the Iran-Iraq War. In response, the United States and several other countries began to implement export controls on chemicals that could be used to manufacture chemical weapons. In 1985, Australia proposed that concerned countries meet in order to coordinate their export controls and share information to enhance their effectiveness. The first meeting took place in June 1985, and biennial meetings continue at the Australian embassy in Paris.

The Australia Group has established a list of chemicals and equipment that are subject to control. In 1990, in response to growing concerns over the proliferation of covert biological weapons programs, certain biological agents and research/production equipment were added to the control list. Australia Group guidelines do not call for prohibiting the export of control list items, but rather establishing monitoring and licensing procedures, with export denial only if there is reason to suspect potential contribution to a CBW program. The Group's list does not curtail legitimate trade.

As noted, the Australia Group does not have an independent administrative organization [http://www.australiagroup.net/index_en.htm]. National governments administer their own export control programs. As an informal effort, it is not based on international treaty, is not affiliated with any international organization, and has no independent administrative structure. It operates entirely upon consensus of its 33 members [http://www.australiagroup.net/agpart.htm](see Appendix A), and its decisions are not binding.

Organization for the Prohibition of Chemical Weapons (OPCW)

The OPCW is headquartered in The Hague. It has four components:

- Conference of States Parties - Comprises all nations who have ratified the Convention; meets annually; has the responsibility to ensure compliance and levy sanctions; selects the Executive Council;
- Executive Council - Comprises 41 states parties on a two-year rotation[34]; directs the routine administration of the OPCW;
- Technical Secretariat - Comprises a permanent international work force; administers and monitors treaty compliance (inspections, data collection and assessment);
- Scientific Advisory Board - Comprised of independent experts to advise the OPCW on relevant scientific and technical issues.

U.S. Government Organizations

In the United States, the following offices, among others, participate in administering the CBW export control program, with State serving as the international point of contact:

- Department of Commerce - Under Secretary of Commerce, Bureau of Industry and Security;
- Department of State - Under Secretary for Arms Control and International Security - Bureau of Arms Control administers the CWC and the Bureau of Nonproliferation administers export controls;
- Department of Defense - Deputy Under-Secretary for Technology Security Policy and Counterproliferation;
- The Department of the Treasury oversees U.S. embargoes through its Office of Foreign Assets Control, and enforces export control through the U.S. Customs Service.

---

[34] By virtue of the treaty -prescribed method of selecting rotational members, the United States will always have a seat on the Executive Council.

U.S. Laws[35]

U.S. laws pertaining to chemical and biological weapons proliferation include statutes and executive orders, the most important of which are the Export Administration Act and the Arms Export Control Act. These statutes operate on the principle that licenses are required for the export of certain goods, and that it is government policy to deny such licenses if there is a danger that the items will contribute to CBW proliferation. In addition, bills to implement the Chemical Weapons Convention were introduced in the 103rd Congress (S.2221/H.R. 4849) and the 104th Congress (S. 1732), though none was reported from committee. In the 105tll Congress, implementing legislation was incorporated into the FY1999 Omnibus Appropriations Act, and signed into law October 20, 1998 (P. L 105-277).

Export Administration Act of 1979

(P.L. 96-72, Section 6(m) and 11C, 50 U.S.C. App. 2405m and 2410c). This Act requires a license for the export of dual-use goods or technology that "would directly and substantially" assist CBW proliferation. Under the Act, the Secretary of Commerce maintains a list of such goods. Exports to countries which have entered into an agreement for the control of restricted goods (i.e. Australia Group members) are exempted from licensing requirements. The EAA requires the President to impose procurement and import sanctions on foreign persons who contribute to CBW proliferation through exports.

Arms Export Control Act

Section 81 of the AECA (22 U.S.C. 2798) provides the State Department the authority to maintain licensing of the export of chemical and biological agents and munitions. It also provides criminal penalties for violation and specifies sanctions against foreign persons who contribute to CW or BW proliferation through exports, and against countries which use chemical or biological weapons or make substantial preparations to do so.

---

[35] This section drawn from CRS Report RL 31502, *Nuclear, Biological, Chemical and Missile Proliferation Sanctions: Selected Current Law.*

Chemical and Biological Weapons Control and Warfare Elimination Act of 1991[36]

This Act mandates U.S. sanctions, and encourages international sanctions, against countries that use chemical or biological weapons in violation of international law. *Section 307 (22 U.S.C. 5605)* requires the President to terminate foreign assistance (except humanitarian, food, and agricultural assistance) arms sales and licenses, credits, guarantees, and certain exports to a government of a foreign country that he has determined has used or made substantial preparation to use chemical or biological weapons. Within three months, the President must determine and certify to Congress that the government: is no longer using chemical or biological weapons in violation of international law, is no longer using such weapons against its own people, has provided credible assurances that such behavior will not resume, and is willing to cooperate with U.N. or other international observers to verify that biological and chemical weapons are not still in use. Without this three-month determination, sanctions are required affecting multilateral development bank loans, U.S. bank loans or credits, exports, imports, diplomatic relations, and aviation access to and from the United States. The President may lift the sanctions after a year, and may waive the imposition of these sanctions.

Biological Anti-Terrorism Act of 1989

This Act (P.L. 101-298) implements the Biological Weapons Convention, providing criminal penalties for its violation. It does not amend either the Export Administration Act or the Arms Export Control Act. For other laws and executive orders that apply to biological weapons proliferation and U.S. nonproliferation policy, see the discussion of U.S. Laws in the above section on the Australia Group.

Additional CW/BW Nonproliferation Policy Provisions in Legislation

Recently, Congress has expressed views on CW/BW nonproliferation policy and U.S. government organization to implement those policies in

---

[36] Title III, P.L. 102-182, 22 U.S.C. 5601-5606.

several other laws. CBW-related provisions have been included in the Iran-Iraq Arms Nonproliferation Act of 1992, the Freedom Support Act, and the Cooperative Threat Reduction Act. These and other provisions are listed in Appendix B.

ISSUES FOR 107TH CONGRESS

Australia Group

There are three significant current issues concerning the Australia Group: (1) expansion of membership; (2) possible transhipment of restricted commodities through AG members; and (3) the AG's relationship to the Chemical Weapons Convention.

The question of membership expansion has been a perennial one, as countries seek AG membership to avoid the export controls imposed on non-members. The AG has remained relatively small because of its inclusion only of countries seriously dedicated to CBW non-proliferation and capable of maintaining an effective export control regime. Some have argued that extending membership to countries such as Russia could provide greater leverage in encouraging export control improvements. To date, however, AG members have not been persuaded that the advantages of such action outweigh the potential for dilution of the regime's effectiveness and new obstacles to consensus-building.

The transhipment issue arises because AG members are exempted from the export licensing requirements for restricted goods and technology. Member states assume that exports to AG members will be controlled by the receiving nation's export control regime once in that country and therefore are not subject to unauthorized reshipment. Critics of this exemption maintain that, in practice, monitoring unlicensed shipments is almost impossible, and that countries such as Iran and Iraq have been able to elude export controls through multiple transshipments. This controversy reflects the perpetual tension between nonproliferation controls and the desire for unfettered commerce with major trading partners.

The question of the Australia Group's relationship to the Chemical Weapons Convention revolves around the Convention's Article XI which declares that states parties will not maintain among themselves any restrictions, including those in any international agreements, incompatible with the obligations undertaken under this Convention, which would restrict or impede trade and the development and promotion of scientific and technological knowledge The Australia Group maintains that its export control regime is compatible with

the objectives of the Convention, and therefore not prohibited. All AG members have agreed, however, to review their export controls to ensure they are consistent with the Convention. A number of developing countries, led by Iran (a CWC signatory), maintain that the AG controls should be dropped - particularly for CWC states parties. They view the controls as a tool of economic oppression on the part of developed countries, even though no country has been able to provide an example where AG controls have resulted in a denial of exports for legitimate purposes. This issue continues to be pressed within the Organization for the Prohibition of Chemical Weapons.

Chemical Weapons Convention

Some provisions of the CWC's implementing legislation (P.L. 105-277) have raised concerns from CWC supporters. These include:

- Section 213 - sets procedures for U.S. firms to seek compensation from the U.S. government, should they suffer the loss of proprietary information through the actions of OPCW employees. Critics, however, maintain that, as worded, this section does not place a high enough burden of proof on the claimants, and consequently could lead to excessive and unfounded claims against the government. To date, no U.S. firm has sought compensation under this provision

- Sections 237 - grants the President the right to deny a request for inspection; if it "may cause a threat to U.S. national security interests." The CWC contains no provision permitting denial of an inspection, and critics note that

- doing so could place the United States in non-compliance. They maintain that even if never exercised, this section's existence will encourage other nations to enact similar exemptions, thereby weakening the CW C verification regime.

- Section 253 exempts discrete organic chemicals not on the CWC control lists and incidental chemical by-products or waste-streams from reporting and inspection requirements. This is intended to ease the potential burdens, particularly on paper manufacturers, but critics believe the exemption is too broadly worded and would rule out an effective non-intrusive sampling technique for inspectors.

In early 2002, the Bush Administration led a successful effort to have Jose Bustani, the Director-General of the OPCW's Technical Secretariat, removed from office. Citing "disdain for the OPCW Executive Committee" and inappropriate administrative and budgetary policies among other charges, the State Department made a concerted and sustained effort to gain support after Bustani refused to voluntarily resign. On April 21, the Conference of OPCW State Parties voted 48-7, with 43 abstentions to support the U.S. position. On July 25, Ambassador Rogelio Pfirter was confirmed the OPCW's new Director-General.

Though the United States attributed the OPCW's fiscal difficulties to DG Bustani's mismanagement, others have pointed to the U.S. and Russia's repeated delinquency in annual dues payments and inspection cost reimbursements as contributing significantly to the OPCW's budget shortfalls. In 2002, the United States refused to support a budget increase to address a backlog of inspections, and was successful in having its pro-rated portion (approximately $15 million) of the annual dues reduced. These actions have raised questions among CWC supporters concerning the U.S. commitment to the OPCW.

Biological Weapons Convention

For most of the 1990s, BWC state parties have sought ways to address the BWC's lack of compliance verification and enforcement provisions. The most extensive effort to draft an adaptation protocol regarding these issues all but collapsed at the last BWC Review Conference in November-December 2002. After six years of negotiation, the United States declared the adaptation protocol draft unacceptable, and rejected it as a basis for further negotiation. In rejecting the draft protocol, the Bush Administration stated that:

The draft Protocol will not improve our ability to verify BWC compliance. It will not enhance our confidence in compliance and will do little to deter those countries seeking to develop biological weapons. In our assessment, the draft Protocol would put national security and confidential business information at risk.[37]

At the same time, the United States introduced a number of proposals which it suggested that nations undertake on a unilateral basis to enhance biological weapons non-proliferation. These were:

- Enact strict national criminal legislation against prohibited BW activities with strong extradition requirements;
- Establish an effective United Nations procedure for investigating suspicious outbreaks or allegations of biological weapons use;
- Establish procedures for addressing BWC compliance concerns;
- Commit to improving international disease control and to enhance mechanisms for sending expert response teams to cope with outbreaks;
- Establish sound national oversight mechanisms for the security and genetic engineering of pathogenic organisms;
- Devise a solid framework for bioscientists in the form of a code of ethical conduct that would have universal recognition; and
- Promote responsible conduct in the study, use, modification, and shipment of pathogenic organisms.

In the wake of the United States statement, the Review Conference was unable to reach consensus on a final conference declaration, and adjourned to reconvene in November 2002. International reaction to the U.S. position has not been generally positive, with many in the arms control community believing that it reflects an attitude of "self-imposed isolation from the mainstream of BWC diplomacy."[38] The developments at the November 2002 Review Conference could be instrumental in determining the future of multilateral biological weapons arms control. There have been no indications that the U.S. position will change substantially, though there will be efforts to put multilateral negotiations back on track. To that end, the United Kingdom has issued a "Green Paper" which it hopes will provide a basis for

---

[37] Statement by the United States to the Ad Hoc Group of Biological Weapons Convention States Parties, Geneva, Switzerland, July 25, 2001.
[38] Sims, Nicholas. "Route-Map to OPBW: Using the Fifth Review Conference," *Chemical and Biological Weapons' Convention Bulletin*. No. 56, June 2002, p. 2

consensus in four areas of concern regarding biological weapons: arms control, preventing supply, deterring use, and defending against use.[39]

As with the CWC, many developing nations, again headed by Iran, are seeking removal of Australia Group controls and increased biotechnical cooperation in exchange for accepting any enhancements to the BWC.

---

[39] *Strengthening the Biological and Toxin Weapons Convention: Countering the Biological Weapons Threat*, Ministry for Foreign and Commonwealth Affairs, London, April 2002 [http://www.brad.ac.uk/acad/sbtwc/other/fcobw.pdf]

Chapter 4

MISSILE PROLIFERATION CONTROL REGIME[40]

In the early 1980s, the United States and its allies became concerned over the rapid spread of missiles as the advanced industrial nations' monopoly on missile technology gave way to a diffusion of missiles and missile technology throughout much of the world. In April 1987, the United States, Canada, France, West Germany, Italy, Japan, and the United Kingdom created the Missile Technology Control Regime (MTCR) to limit the proliferation of missiles capable of delivering nuclear weapons. Thirty-three countries are now partners in the MTCR.[4] In addition, Bulgaria, China, Israel, Romania, and the Slovak Republic have agreed to observe the MTCR guidelines but without becoming partners of the regime. Israel additionally has completed a memorandum of understanding with the United States affirming its commitment to abide by the MTCR guidelines.

The Regime is based on the premise that foreign acquisition and development of missiles can be delayed and made more difficult and expensive if major producers agree to control exports of missiles and the equipment and technology used in missile production. The MTCR is similar in this regard to the Nuclear Suppliers Group, the Australia Group, and the Wassenaar Arrangement. It differs from the nuclear, chemical, and biological non-proliferation regimes in that the MTCR is not supported by a treaty and has no international organization to verify or enforce compliance. Rather, the MTCR is a set of common export control guidelines adopted and administered independently by each of the partner nations.

---

[40] Prepared by Sharon Squassoni, Foreign Affairs, Defense, and Trade Division.
[41] See Appendix A for a list of current partners.

The specific missile equipment and technology subject to the guidelines is described in an annex to the MTCR Guidelines and divided into two categories. Each of the member countries is to exercise particular restraint in considering transfers of items in *Category I* which include complete rocket systems and unmanned air vehicle (UAV) systems capable of delivering a 500-kilogram (1,100-pound) payload to a range of 300 kilometers (186 miles) or more, and complete subsystems of such missiles and vehicles. There is a strong presumption to deny transfers of these systems and components. The guidelines further state the transfer of Category I production facilities will not be authorized. Export restraints are to be applied to Category II items, which consist of other components, equipment, material, and technology that would be usable in the production of missiles and UAVs. Category II also includes, at item number 19, complete rocket systems and UAVs with a 300-km range but not capable of delivering a 500-kg payload to that range (as covered by Category I), and in item number 20, individual rocket stages and rocket engines and production equipment usable for systems with a range of 300 km with less than a 500-kg payload.

In January 1993, MTCR partners revised the guidelines to limit the risks of proliferation of missile delivery systems for all weapons of mass destruction: chemical and biological weapons as well as nuclear weapons. The guidelines now call for particular restraint and the presumption to deny transfers of any missiles (whether or not they are included in the annex) and of any items in the annex if the government judges that they are intended to be used for the delivery of weapons of mass destruction.[42] This addition is commonly referred to as a "catch-all" clause.

The MTCR has undergone a transformation from a small group of Western industrial countries to a more inclusive group of countries. Argentina, with its Condor II missile program, was originally one of the primary targets of the Regime, but it terminated development of Condor II and is now a full partner in the MTCR. South Africa and Brazil had active missile programs but are now partners. Whereas the Soviet Union was the

---

[42] According to the guidelines, the government judgment on the likely use of the missile items will be made, "on the basis of all available, persuasive information, evaluated according to factors including . . .
   (A) Concerns about the proliferation of weapons of mass destruction;
   (B) The capabilities and objectives of the missile and space programs of the recipient state;
   (C) The significance of the transfer in terms of the potential development of delivery systems (other than manned aircraft) for weapons of mass destruction;
   (D) The assessment of the end-use of the transfers, including the relevant assurances of the recipient states; and
   (E) The applicability of relevant multilateral agreements."

primary source for missiles to the Third World in the 1970s and 1980s, Russia has become a partner in the MTCR, although the United States has sanctioned Russian organizations for improper exports to Iran. China has been, and still is, another significant supplier of missiles and missile technology to developing countries but committed to observing the MTCR guidelines and pledged not to transfer surface-to-surface missiles that meet the MTCR thresholds. In spite of these commitments, Russian and Chinese organizations and individuals continue to supply components and technical assistance for missile production.

North Korea has become the primary supplier of missiles and missile technology to developing countries. Iran, Iraq, Libya, Syria, India, and Pakistan are the other countries of major concern regarding the development and acquisition of missiles. Missile programs in China, Egypt, and South Korea have also caused concern in Washington. Cruise missiles have always been included with ballistic missiles and space-launch vehicles in the MTCR but are now receiving greater attention as advanced propulsion and guidance technology is becoming more widely available.

The United States has stated its support for expanding membership of the MTCR, "to include additional countries that subscribe to international non- proliferation standards, enforce effective export controls, and abandon offensive ballistic missile programs."[43] The United States will not support space launch programs in non-MTCR countries but will consider exports of MTCR items for use in space-launch programs by MTCR countries on a case-by-case basis. The United States and other MTCR countries are promoting regional efforts to reduce the demand for missiles and persuade countries to forgo the acquisition of missiles.

Some nations have not joined the MTCR; affirming their sovereign right to acquire, develop, deploy, and export missiles. Particular difficulties have been encountered in controlling dual-use technologies which may be used for civilian space launch vehicles, civil aviation, general industry, and tactical weapons, as well as for actual missile delivery systems for nuclear, chemical or biological weapons. MTCR member states have been working since about 1999 on a complementary effort which has become known as the International Code of Conduct (ICOC) Against Ballistic Missile Proliferation. A draft agreement emerged in early 2002, which included broad principles, general commitments and modest confidence-building

---

[43] U.S. Department of State. Reprint of White House Press Release, Non-Proliferation and Export Control Policy, September 27, 1993.

measures. More than 75 states attended the February 2002 meeting to discuss the draft code of conduct; almost 100 states attended the June 2002 meeting.

The United States supports the development of the code, which attempts to fill the gap of demand-side incentives by offering "cooperation" with respect to civilian space-launch vehicle technology in exchange for significant nonproliferation commitments. However, such cooperation is to be worked out between states and is not specified in the draft document. Therefore, the incentives for cooperation appear to be elusive thus far.

IMPLEMENTING THE REGIME

International Organization

While the MTCR has no international organization, partner countries hold monthly meetings in Paris among embassy representatives (called "points of contact" meetings), hold technical experts' meetings (including information exchanges) and convene a plenary once each year. In this manner, partners revise the guidelines and the equipment annex and admit new partners.

U.S. Government Organization

In the United States, the Office of Defense Trade Controls of the State Department administers the regulations governing the export of items on the Munitions List - those items that are subject to controls under the AECA and the ITAR. The Bureau of Industry and Security (formerly Bureau of Export Administration) in the U.S. Department of Commerce administers the regulations governing the export of items on the Commerce Control List - those items that are primarily for civilian use but have applications for the development, testing, or production of missiles.

The Missile Technology Export Control Committee is an interagency group, chaired by an official of the State Department, that reviews controversial missile export license cases. The Missile Trade Analysis Group, another interagency group chaired by a State Department representative, reviews intelligence reports on diversions of missile technology from legitimate recipients to others.

Officials in the State Department's Bureau of Nonproliferation and regional bureaus also undertake diplomatic initiatives to dissuade additional nations from developing missiles, to persuade other countries to adopt export controls on missile technology, and to reduce the perceived need for missiles.

Department of Defense officials have established a counter-proliferation policy that addresses export controls, security relationships with friendly and hostile countries, defensive and offensive military operational concepts, and equipment. Many organizations within the Department implement the various aspects of the counter-proliferation policy, but the Assistant Secretary for International Security Policy has the primary responsibility for counter-proliferation policy formulation.

The Department of the Treasury also oversees U.S. embargoes through its Office of Foreign Assets Control, and helps enforce export controls through the U.S. Customs Service.

U.S. Laws[44]

The United States has maintained stringent controls on missiles and missile technology under the Arms Export Control Act (22 V.S.C. 2751) and the International Traffic in Arms Regulations (22 C.F.R. Part 121, hereafter the ITAR).

In the early 1980s, the United States also unilaterally adopted tighter export controls on dual-use equipment and technology that could benefit foreign missile programs. Dual-use controls have been placed in the Export Administration Regulations (15 C.F.R. 730-799) pursuant to the authority of the Export Administration Act of 1979 (50 U.S.C. app. 2401 et seq.) and the International Emergency Economic Powers Act (50- U.S.C. 1701 et seq.). Successive administrations have updated regulations to reflect changes adopted by the MTCR, changes in U.S. law, and the changing international political environment. The Export Administration Act of 1979 has expired several times, but the President has invoked his authority to continue in effect the system of controls that had been maintained under the act.

Members of Congress became interested in missile proliferation in the mid-1980s because of evidence of Third World missile development and acquisition programs and because the developing threat was an additional consideration in funding the Strategic Defense Initiative (SDI, a Reagan-era program that funded research into ballistic missile defenses). Libya had purchased Soviet Scud missiles and Iran and Iraq were firing missiles at each other. Congress had little or no involvement in shaping the MTCR, since it was neither a treaty nor an executive agreement. Soon after the Regime was announced in April 1987, it became apparent that companies and individuals from a number of MTCR member countries (such as West Germany, Italy, Britain, and France) were transferring goods and technical assistance to missile development teams in Argentina, Brazil, Iraq, Egypt, and elsewhere. In 1987, the United States also learned that China had transferred intermediate range missiles to Saudi Arabia. Many Members of Congress thought the MTCR needed enforcement mechanisms, additional members, and stricter compliance.

Several bills were introduced in the 101st Congress with the intention of strengthening the U.S. position on missile nonproliferation. Several bills that included sanctions against nations, companies, and individuals who violate the MTCR guidelines gained widespread bipartisan congressional support. Bush Administration officials maintained that the President already had sufficient authority to reprimand or sanction foreign governments, companies, and individuals for inappropriate missile transfers and objected to the imposition of mandatory statutory sanctions. President Bush pocket vetoed the Export Administration Act of 1990, which included a missile nonproliferation provision, as well as the Chemical and Biological Weapons Control Act. However, he signed the defense authorization bill that contained a nearly identical section on missile nonproliferation policy.

The Missile Technology Control Act of 1990

The Act became law in the 101st Congress (H.R. 4739, Title XVII of the National Defense Authorization Act for Fiscal Year 1991, P.L. 101-510). It added Chapter 7 to the Arms Export Control Act, sections 6(1) and 11B to the Export Administration Act of 1979, and established an annual reporting requirement. Chapter 7 of the AECA has been amended several times.

The Arms Export Control Act

(22 U.S.C. 2751 et seq.) Chapter 7 of the AECA requires the President to impose sanctions on U.S. and foreign individuals who improperly conduct trade in controlled missile technology. If a person inappropriately transfers

---

[44] *This section drawn from CRS Report RL35102,*Nuclear, Biological, Chemical and Missile Proliferation Sanctions: Selected Current Law.

MTCR Category II goods or technology, he/she will be denied, for two years, any U.S. Government contracts relating to missile equipment or technology, and U.S. export licenses for missile equipment and technology. The AECA requires sanctions for at least two years if a person inappropriately transfers Category I items; these include denial of all U.S. Government contracts and export licenses for any item on the U.S. Munitions List. If the President determines that a foreign person has substantially contributed to the design, development, or production of missiles by a non-MTCR country, he shall prohibit for at least two years U.S. imports of items produced by that person. The Act includes presidential waivers, exclusions, determination requirements, and definitions that allow the Administration to take no action in certain circumstances.

These sanctions may be waived by the President, and they generally do not apply to transfers of missile goods or technology to an MTCR adherent or from an MTCR adherent. The United States has imposed missile sanctions against entities in several countries including China, Pakistan, South Africa, North Korea, Iran, Russia, India, Syria, and Egypt

The Export Administration Act of 1979

(Sections 6 (1) and 11B, 50 U.S.C. app. 2405 and app. 2410b). Similarly, the EAA requires controls on U.S. missile-related exports and sanctions against U.S. and foreign persons who improperly transfer dual-use goods or technology listed in the MTCR annex. If a person improperly transfers Category II goods or technology, he will be denied export licenses for two years for missile equipment and technology controlled under the EAA. If a person improperly exports Category I goods or technology, he will be denied export licenses for at least two years for all items controlled under the EAA. If a foreign person exports goods or technology that substantially contribute to the design, development, or production of missiles in a non-MTCR country, he will be denied license to import his products into the United States for at least two years. Actions that trigger sanctions under the provisions of either the AECA or the EAA, require commensurate sanctions under the other act.

Additional Missile Nonproliferation Policy Provisions in Legislation

Over the years, Congress has called for additional sanctions, expressed views on nonproliferation policies related to missiles or advanced conventional weapons, and expressed views on the organization of the U.S. Government to implement those policies in several other laws. There are provisions related to missile proliferation in the Foreign Assistance Act of 1961, the Iran Nonproliferation Act of 2000, the Iran-Iraq Arms Nonproliferation Act of 1992, the Freedom Support Act, and the Cooperative Threat Reduction Act. These and other laws are listed in Appendix B.

ISSUES FOR 107TH CONGRESS

A perennial problem is whether the MTCR and the associated U.S. sanctions are effective enough to warrant the economic and political costs to the United States, and whether additional or alternative feasible measures would increase effectiveness.

Many analysts consider the MTCR a successful vehicle of quiet diplomacy. The MTCR has been credited with slowing missile development in Brazil and India, and blocking a collaborative program of Argentina, Egypt, and Iraq to build the Condor missile. This missile would have been a significant improvement over the Scud-based missiles used by Iraq in the Gulf War. Russia and China have probably stopped exporting entire missiles that fall under the parameters of the MTCR, but continue to transfer components and technology. Most European countries and Asian allies have tightened their export control laws and some have prosecuted individuals who have smuggled missile technology as well as nuclear and chemical production technology. Accurate long-range missiles are expensive and difficult to develop and produce. Because most countries cannot produce and integrate all of the sophisticated components required, the MTCR and complementary export control systems will probably continue to impede Third World development of the most advanced missiles.

However, much of the international commerce in missiles and missile technology occurs between nations that do not adhere to MTCR guidelines. China and North Korea are not members, although China promised to observe the guidelines after the United States had twice imposed economic sanctions on Chinese companies for transferring missile items to Pakistan, on the condition that the United States would lift those sanctions. North

Korea's missile development, production, deployment, and export of missiles has apparently not been hindered by the MTCR. In particular, North Korean exports of missile production technology to Iran, Pakistan, Syria, Egypt, and perhaps Libya seriously undercut the international standards and goals of the Regime. In the view of some analysts, the activities of North Korea demonstrate the failure of the MTCR.

Some difficulties associated with the nuclear, chemical, and biological nonproliferation regimes may be even more acute with respect to missile technology. The notion of a suppliers' regime dividing the world into "haves" and have-nots" is even more exacerbated in the case of missiles, since there is no treaty and no *quid pro quo* for the have-nots. The International Code of Conduct is an attempt to address this "carrot" side of the carrot-stick equation, but is considered by some observers to be altogether too vague as an incentive and by other observers as too vague and therefore too expansive. Also, there is a common perception that technology is shared among MTCR members, although the guidelines call for the strong presumption of denial of Category I-class missiles and technology to anyone. The recent U.S. decision to elaborate what constitutes "rare occasions" (wherein Category I presumption of denials could be overruled) lends credence to this view.[45]

Further, while many of the materials associated with nuclear weapons can be identified and controlled, the materials and components used in missiles are commonly used in a wide range of commercial manufacturing processes. Ballistic missiles can be nearly indistinguishable from civilian space launch vehicles, and some missile production equipment, technology, and materials are difficult to distinguish from civilian items. This is particularly acute in the case of UAVs.

As developing nations become increasingly capable of producing missiles indigenously, the effectiveness of supplier controls is gradually being eroded. A growing list of nations now produce ballistic missiles and are increasingly less dependent on imported materials. Some analysts see attempts to control missile technology exports as futile and argue for the fewest export restrictions possible, emphasizing the importance to the U.S. economy of exports. Others say the U.S. Government should not allow the export of any goods that are likely to harm U.S. national security, despite the potential effect on some American business interests.

---

[45] Testimony given by Vann Van Diepen, Deputy Assistant Secretary of State for Proliferation Controls in a hearing before Senate Government Affairs Committee, Subcommittee on International Security, Proliferation and Federal Services, June 11, 2002.

In addition to the promotion of exports, other foreign policy and national security goals may also compete with missile nonproliferation for priority of government attention and action. For instance, U.S. leaders hope to encourage Russia and China to become stable and responsible actors in their regions and in the international community, to pursue economic and political reforms, and to respect internationally recognized human rights. The United States seeks the cooperation of those two countries and many others in efforts to block nuclear proliferation, terrorism, drug trafficking, and organized crime. Although missile nonproliferation will remain an issue of utmost importance, other goals may occasionally be given greater emphasis. However, when political leaders suspend missile nonproliferation policies in favor of other goals, the credibility of the U.S. missile policy and that of the MTCR are damaged. It can become more difficult to persuade other countries to comply with a set of standards when the United States appears to enforce the . standards on a selective basis. The priority to be given to missile nonproliferation has occasionally been a point of contention between Congress and the administration.

Congress has established economic sanctions that must be imposed on companies that trade in missile technology contrary to the MTCR guidelines. The imposition, lifting, and waiving of these sanctions frequently cause controversy. Some analysts suggest these negative actions should be coupled with positive incentives to induce countries to refrain from proliferation. Positive incentives could include trade credits, development assistance, military assistance, technology transfers, access to space launch and satellite capabilities, or security guarantees. But other analysts contend the security benefits derived from adhering to the MTCR should be sufficient and that the United States should not try to buy compliance.

According to many foreign policy specialists, the underlying political and security problems that drive proliferation must be resolved before meaningful curbs can be applied to the spread of weapons of mass destruction and missiles. The United States and its partners in the MTCR have helped countries, particularly neighbors in regions of ongoing conflict, to adopt confidence-building measures such as those that have contributed to security and cooperation in Europe. They also try to help correct regional imbalance of military forces and to facilitate peace negotiations and arms control talks.

Security alliances and military assistance can play a role in restraining missile development. The U.S. security umbrella over Western Europe and parts of Asia and the transfer of large quantities of advanced conventional weapons helped to dissuade a number of U.S. allies from developing weapons of mass destruction and helped deter aggression. Some analysts contend that the security of some allies was enhanced by the deterrent power of U.S. nuclear-armed missiles previously deployed in their territory or, possibly in the case of Israel, by indigenous weapons. The U.S. Government has also decided that it is appropriate to sell missiles (U.S. Army Tactical Missile Systems) with a potential range of 250 km to Turkey, Greece, South Korea, Britain, France, and Germany, though it forbids sales of missiles with a range of 300 km. However, the superiority of U.S. military technology may actually persuade some adversary countries to develop weapons of mass destruction and missiles as their best means of deterring U.S. intervention.

Some analysts see missile defense systems as a proper alternative to export controls, though most see them as supplementary to other military, political, and economic measures (including export controls and sanctions). The United States will probably deploy theater and national missile defense systems and has provided defensive missiles to some allies in Europe, East Asia, and the Mid-East. As the United States seeks to increase defense cooperation in the area of missile defenses, issues could arise about the applicability of MTCR guidelines. One particular recent case where questions have arisen is the proposed transfer of Arrow missile defense systems from Israel to India.[46] Air defense missiles and anti-theater ballistic missiles probably enhance the security of U.S. allies, but none are expected to be 100 percent effective. In some cases, such as Taiwan, deployments might increase tensions. The Administration and Congress will have to weigh carefully defense policy objectives against nonproliferation policy objectives in this area.

---

[46] In a hearing on Multilateral Nonproliferation Regimes of the International Security, Proliferation and Federal Services Subcommittee of the Senate Governmental Affairs Committee, July 29, 2002, Vann Van Diepen, Deputy Assistant Secretary of State for Proliferation Controls, stated that the Arrow interceptor is a MTCR Category-1 class missile and that Israel would have to go through the necessary procedures to decide it could overcome a strong presumption of denial to make such a sale.

Chapter 5

APPENDIX A. PROLIFERATION CONTROL REGIME MEMBERSHIP

Nuclear Suppliers Groups (38)	MTCR (33)	Australia Group (33)
Argentina*	Argentina	Argentina
Australia *	Australia	Australia
Austria *	Austria	Austria
Belarus		
Belgium*	Belgium	Belgium
Brazil	Brazil	
Bulgaria*		Bulgaria
Canada*	Canada	Canada
Cyprus		Cyprus
Czech Republic*	Czech Republic	Czech Republic
Denmark*	Denmark	Denmark
Finland *	Finland	Finland
France *	France	France
Germany *	Germany	Germany
Greece*	Greece	Greece
Hungary *	Hungary	Hungary
	Iceland	Iceland
Ireland *	Ireland	Ireland
Italy*	Italy	Italy
Japan *	Japan	Japan
Latvia		

Nuclear Suppliers Groups (38)	MTCR (33)	Australia Group (33)
Luxembourg *	Luxembourg	Luxembourg
Netherlands	Netherlands	Netherlands
New Zealand	New Zealand	New Zealand
Norway *	Norway	Norway
Poland *	Poland	Poland
Portugal *	Portugal	Portugal
Romania *		Romania
Russia *	Russia	
Slovakia*		Slovakia
South Africa *	South Africa	
South Korea*	South Korea	South Korea
Spain *	Spain	Spain
Sweden*	Sweden	Sweden
Switzerland*	Switzerland	Switzerland
Turkey	Turkey	Turkey
Ukraine	Ukraine	
United Kingdom*	United Kingdom	United Kingdom
United States*	United States	United States

* Denotes 31 countries also members of the Zangger Committee. China is also a member of the Zangger Committee but not the NSG.

Chapter 6

APPENDIX B. ADDITIONAL LEGISLATION AND EXECUTIVE ORDERS

Combating Proliferation of Weapons of Mass Destruction Act of 1996, Title VII, Intelligence Authorization Act for Fiscal Year 1997, P. L 104-293, 50, U.S.C. 2301 note.

National Defense Authorization Act for Fiscal Year 1994, Title XVI, Arms Control Matters, Nonproliferation Provisions, P. L. 103-160.

National Defense Authorization Act for Fiscal Year 1995, Title XV, Arms Control Matters, Nonproliferation Provisions, P. L. 103-337; 22 U.S.C. 2751 note.

Weapons of Mass Destruction Control Act of 1992, Title XV, National Defense Authorization Act for Fiscal Year 1993, P. L. 102-484; 22 U.S.C. 5859a begins at section 1505 of Act.

Antiterrorism and Effective Death Penalty Act of 1996, Title V, Nuclear, Biological, and Chemical Weapons Restrictions, P .L. 104-132, 18 U.S.C. 831 note, and 2331, 42 U.S.C. 262 note, 50 U.S.C. 1522 note.

Arms Control and Nonproliferation Act of 1994, Title VIII, Part A, Foreign Relations Authorization Act, Fiscal Years 1994 and 1995, P.L. 103-236, 22 V.S.C. 2551 note.

Defense Against Weapons of Mass Destruction Act of 1996, Title XIV, National Defense Authorization Act for Fiscal Year 1997, P .L. 104-201, 50 U.S.C. 2301 note.

Executive Order 13222 (August 17, 2001, 66 FR 44025, August 22, 2001 Continuation of Export Control Regulations.

Continued on August 15, 2002 by notice published in Federal Register on August 16, 2002.

Executive Order 13049 (June 11, 1997,62 FR 32471) Organization for the Prohibition of Chemical Weapons.

Executive Order 13030 Administration of Foreign Assistance and Arms Exports (December 12, 1996, 61 FR 66187).

Executive Order 12938 (Nov. 14, 1994,59 F.R. 59-9,50 U.S.C. 1701 note) Declares the proliferation of weapons of mass destruction and their means of delivery as an unusual and extraordinary threat and declares a national emergency to deal with that threat.

Amended by EO 13094 (July 28, 1998, 63 FR40803 and by EO 13128 (June 25, 1999, 64 FR 34703).

Executive Order 12946 (Jan. 20,1995,60 F.R. 4829, 22 U.S.C. 2551 note) "Establishes the President's Advisory Board on Arms Proliferation Policy.

Executive Order 12851 (June 11, 1993, 58 F.R. 33181, 22 U.S.C. 2797 note) Delegates President's authority under the Export Administration Act, Arms Control Export Act, and the Chemical and Biological Weapons Control, Warfare Elimination Act, National Defense Authorization Act for Fiscal Years 1992 and 1993, National Defense Authorization Act for Fiscal Year 1993, and Foreign Relations Authorizations Act for Fiscal Years 1992 and 1993, to the Secretaries of State, Commerce, Defense, and Treasury, and Director of ACDA.

Executive Order 11850 (April 8, 1975,40 F.R. 16187,50 U.S.C. 1511 note) Renunciation of certain uses in war of chemical herbicides and riot control agents.

INDEX

A

Africa, 14, 17, 22, 24, 48, 53, 60
African Nuclear Weapon-Free-Zone Treaty, 17
allied troops, 25
American business interests, 55
Anti-Ballistic Missile (ABM), 3, 20
anti-theater ballistic missiles, 57
arms control, 2-4, 15, 33, 36, 44, 56
Arms Export Control Act (AECA), 6-10, 26, 27, 29-31, 39, 40, 50-53
Atomic Energy Act (AEA), 5, 7, 9, 26
Atomic Energy Commission, 15, 26
Australia Group (AG), 2, 7, 37, 39-42, 45, 47, 59

B

ballistic missile defenses, 51
Belarus, 3, 14, 59
bilateral diplomatic agreements, vii, 13
Biological (and Toxin) Weapons Convention (BWC), 7, 10, 35-37, 40, 43-45
Biological Anti-Terrorism Act, 10, 40
biological weapons, vii, 1, 27, 37, 39, 40, 43, 44, 49
biotechnical cooperation, 45
bombs, 13, 18
Brazil, 6, 14, 17, 24, 48, 52, 54, 59
Britain, 13, 15, 17, 52, 57
Bulgaria, 47, 59
Bush Administration, 20, 25, 43, 52
Bush, President, 20, 22, 29, 31, 52

C

Canada, 15, 19, 47, 59
Carter Administration, 26
Cenral Intelligence Agency (CIA), 25
chemical and biological agents/weapons, vii, 1, 2, 6, 13, 39, 48
Chemical and Biological Weapons Control Act, 52
Chemical Weapons Convention (CWC), 3, 7, 10, 35-39, 41-43, 45
chemical weapons, 25, 27, 35-37, 40
Chile, 17
China, 2, 3, 13, 15, 17, 18, 21, 24, 47, 49, 52-54, 56, 60
civil and military applications, 23
Clinton, President, 20
coercive measures, 1

Comprehensive Test Ban Treaty (CTBT), 3, 19, 20
control list items, 37
Convention on the Physical Protection of Nuclear Material, 14, 16
Convention on the Protection of Physical Security, 22
Cooperative Threat Reduction programs, 25, 33
counterproliferation, 1, 5, 25
counterterrorism, 19

D

Department of Commerce, 25, 38, 50
Department of Defense (DoD), 25, 31-33, 38, 51
Department of Energy (DoE), 25-27, 32
Department of State, 25, 38, 50
Department of the Treasury, 25, 38, 51
destructive uses, 15
diplomatic relations, 40
disarmament, 16, 19, 20
domestic agencies, vii, 13

E

enforcement mechanisms, 2, 52
Export Administration Act (EAA), 6-10, 29, 30, 39, 40, 51-53, 62
export controls, 2, 3, 5, 21, 23, 24, 29, 37, 38, 41, 42, 49, 51, 57
Export-Import Bank Act (Ex-Im Bank), 7, 9, 30
exports, 2-4, 6, 23, 25-31, 39-42, 47, 49, 53, 55, 56

F

Foreign Assistance Act, 26, 29, 54
foreign assistance, 40

Foreign Corrupt Practices Act, 30
foreign country, 26, 40
foreign policy considerations, 27, 29
former Soviet republics, 14
France, 13, 15, 17, 47, 52, 57, 59

G

Germany, 14, 57, 59
Global Partnership, 3, 15, 19
Greece, 57, 59
Gulf War, 5, 24, 54

H

Hiroshima, 15

I

imports, 30, 40, 53
India, 3, 13-15, 23, 24, 31, 33, 49, 53, 54, 57
International Atomic Energy Agency (IAEA), 7, 14-16, 18, 21, 22, 24, 27, 33
International Code of Conduct (ICOC), 8, 49, 55
international consensus, vii, 1
International Emergency Economic Powers Act, 30, 51
International Peace Conferences, 35
international standards, 1, 16, 55
international terrorism, 28, 29
Iran, 3, 6-8, 10, 11, 14, 24, 32, 33, 37, 41, 42, 45, 49, 51, 53-55
Iraq, 2, 3, 5-8, 10, 14, 15, 22-25, 32, 37, 41, 49, 51, 54
Israel, 13-15, 24, 47, 57
Italy, 47, 52, 59

J

Japan, 14, 19, 47, 59

Index

K

Kazakhstan, 3, 14
Kennedy, President, 13
Korean Peninsula Energy Development Organization (KEDO), 19

L

Latin America, 17
Libya, 3, 14, 49, 51, 55

M

military operations, 1
missile defenses, 3, 5, 57
missile nonproliferation policy, 52
missile production, 47, 49, 55
missile proliferation, 2, 4, 51, 54
missile regime, 1
Missile Technology Control Regime (MTCR), 2, 8, 47-57, 59
missiles, vii, 1, 4, 6, 13, 27, 31, 47-51, 53-57
MTCR guidelines, 47, 49
multilateral organizations, vii, 1, 13
munitions, 5, 28, 39

N

Nagasaki, 15
national laws, 1
National Security Council, 24
Netherlands, 17, 60
Newly Independent States (NIS), 6, 10, 18, 31, 33
non-nuclear-weapon-state(s), 14-16, 19, 27, 28
nonproliferation and counterproliferation objectives, 1
nonproliferation regime, vii, 13, 15, 25, 37

North Korea, 3, 13-15, 18, 19, 22, 33, 49, 53, 54
nuclear age, vii, 13
nuclear detonations, vii
nuclear device, 27, 29
nuclear energy, 5, 15, 16, 21, 26
nuclear explosive devices, 27, 28
nuclear exports, 23, 24, 25, 27, 33
nuclear material(s), 14-16, 20, 21, 23, 26-28, 30, 31, 33
Nuclear Non-Proliferation Act (NNPA), 7, 9, 25-27
nuclear nonproliferation regime, vii, 3, 13, 20, 21, 35
Nuclear Nonproliferation Treaty (NPT), 3, 6, 7, 14-16, 18, 19, 21-23, 33
nuclear nonproliferation, vii, 1, 3, 13, 15, 18, 20, 21, 26, 27, 29, 33, 35
Nuclear Posture Review, 20
nuclear program(s), 14, 16, 26, 33
Nuclear Proliferation Prevention Act, 10, 29, 30
nuclear proliferation, 14, 27, 28, 30, 31, 33, 56
Nuclear Regulatory Commission, 25, 26
Nuclear Suppliers Group (NSG), 2, 23, 24, 27, 33, 47, 60
nuclear weapons, vii, 1, 3, 5, 13-15, 17, 19, 20, 24-26, 28, 30, 31, 33, 35, 47, 48, 55
nuclear-weapon(s) free zone (NWFZ), 17, 18
nuclear-weapon-states, 15, 16, 19
Nunn-Lugar Amendment, 31

O

Office of Foreign Assets Control, 25, 38, 51
Organization for the Prohibition of Chemical Weapons (OPCW), 7, 36-38, 42, 43, 62

P

Pakistan, 6, 13-15, 24, 29, 31, 33, 49, 53, 54
peace negotiations, 56
plutonium, 1, 13, 18, 19, 26, 33
potential terrorist access, 3
presidential waiver, 11, 30
Pressler amendment, 29
production equipment, 37, 48
Putin, President, 20

Q

quid pro quo, 19, 21, 55

R

radiological devices, 22
Reagan-era program, 51
Related Arms Control Agreements, 19
rocket engines, 48
Romania, 47, 60
Russia, 2, 3, 6, 9-11, 13, 15, 17-19, 31, 33, 41, 43, 49, 53, 54, 56, 60

S

safeguards violations, 18
sanctions, 4, 5, 6, 9, 28, 31, 32, 38-40, 52-54, 56, 57
Second World War, 14
Security Assistance Act, 29
security conditions, 2, 4
September 11th, 3, 14, 22, 25, 31, 32
South Korea, 6, 14, 19, 49, 57, 60
South Pacific, 17
Southeast Asia, 17, 18
Soviet Scud missiles, 51
Soviet Union, 5, 14, 18, 22, 25, 48
State Department, 24, 26, 29, 32, 37, 39, 43, 50
statutory authority, 1, 2
Strategic Defense Initiative (SDI), 51

T

terrorism, 16, 28, 31, 32, 56
terrorist attacks, 14, 31
Treaty of Bangkok, 7, 18
Treaty of Moscow, 7, 20
Treaty of Pelindaba, 7, 17
Treaty of Rarotonga, 7, 17
Treaty of Tlatelolco, 7, 17
Turkey, 57, 60

U

U.S. Army Tactical Missile Systems, 57
U.S. Customs Service, 25, 38, 51
U.S. embargoes, 25, 38, 51
U.S. Munitions List, 28, 53
Ukraine, 3, 14, 60
underlying motivations, 2, 4
United Kingdom, 44, 47, 60
United Nations, 18, 21, 37, 44
unmanned air vehicle(s) (UAV(s)), 48, 55
uranium, 1, 26

W

Wassenaar Arrangement, 47
weapons development, 14, 23
weapons of mass destruction (WMD), vii, 2-4, 6, 14, 15, 19, 22, 25, 29, 32, 33, 48, 56, 57, 62
weapons states, 3, 13, 15, 17, 18
West Germany, 47, 52
WMD proliferation, 4, 6, 29
Wolf, Secretary of State for Nonproliferation John S., 4
World War I, 35